# WILD WOODS

*For my grandchildren,*
*Ivy, Iris and Robyn*

# WILD WOODS

## THE MAGIC OF IRELAND'S NATIVE WOODLANDS

## RICHARD NAIRN

*GILL BOOKS*

Gill Books
Hume Avenue
Park West
Dublin 12
www.gillbooks.ie

Gill Books is an imprint of M.H. Gill and Co.

© Richard Nairn 2020
978 07171 9021 8

Photos © Richard Nairn, except where stated

The author and publisher thank Coillte Nature for its
support towards the publication of this book.

Edited by Sheila Armstrong
Proofread by Neil Burkey
Printed by CPI Group (UK) Ltd, Croydon, CRO 4YY

This book is typeset in 12.5 on 21pt, Sabon.
The paper used in this book comes from the wood pulp of
managed forests. For every tree felled, at least one tree is
planted, thereby renewing natural resources.

5 4 3 2

# *Contents*

## About the Author

Richard Nairn is an ecologist and writer who has spent a lifetime studying nature. He is an advocate of nature conservation and lectures regularly. During his career, he has worked as a nature reserve warden and was the first Director of BirdWatch Ireland. He is a scientific advisor to Woodlands of Ireland and the author of numerous books.

## Also by Richard Nairn

*Wild Wicklow: Nature in the Garden of Ireland*
*Ireland's Coastline: Exploring its Nature and Heritage*
*Bird Habitats in Ireland* (joint editor)
*Dublin Bay: Nature and History*

*Preface*

The final parts of this book were written in 2020 during the Coronavirus pandemic that swept across the world, stopping a lot of normal human activity in its tracks. My usual work was suspended, travel was restricted to local journeys only and I found myself largely confined to my home place.

But nature continued pretty much as usual. Primroses flowered in spring, hazel catkins glowed yellow at dawn, the first swallows appeared on the same date as the previous year and the sun shone each day of that early summer. The familiarity of nature's seasons was more than reassuring. My daily routine slowed and every day seemed to be the same. I left my mobile phone at home and spent much more time that year alone in our woodland, planting trees, chopping logs and just observing nature around me. I cooked meals on an open wood fire and I sat for hours by the river, listening to birdsong and the rustling of the leaves. The wood gave me the sanctuary that I needed as the world outside was consumed by a deadly illness. I learnt the true value of nature to the human soul.

The book has benefitted from information, photographs and guidance generously provided by Michael Carey, Mike Carswell, John Cross, Joanne Denyer, Paul Dowding, Katharine Duff, Shirley Gleeson, Amber Godwin, Joe Gowran, Ciara Hamilton, Clare Heardman, Matthew Jebb, Colin Kelleher, Daniel Kelly, Mary Kelly-Quinn, Ian Killeen, Declan Little, Coilin Maclochlainn, Evelyn Moorkens, Declan Murphy, Derry Nairn, Tim Nairn, Will O'Connor, Christian Osthoff, Karl Partridge, Paddy Purser, Jenni Roche, Tim Roderick, Marc Ruddock, Liz Sheppard, Ralph Sheppard, Courtney Tyler, Angus Tyner and Paddy Woodworth. Members of Woodlands of Ireland have provided much stimulation and discussion about all aspects of native woodlands that prompted many of the ideas in this book.

I would like to acknowledge Bloodaxe Books for permission to reproduce the poem 'When the Tree Falls' by Jane Clarke. I also acknowledge Faber & Faber for permission to reproduce an extract from 'Blackberry Picking' by Seamus Heaney. My thanks are due to Margaret Connolly. Her excellent local history of a neighbouring townland called *Aghowle* gave me the factual context for describing the lives of previous owners of our land, who themselves are fictitious with no connection to any living person.

Coillte Nature* is acknowledged for supporting the publication of this book, which I hope will be helpful in their valuable work. Declan Little read the entire manuscript and made many useful suggestions for its improvement. The editor Sheila Armstrong kept the whole project on track and helped me turn the science into readable form.

Last but not least, I am thankful for the support of my wife, Wendy, and our family in the exciting project we have taken on together to manage our land in a more sustainable way into the future.

---

*Note: Coillte Nature is the non-profit branch of Coillte that is dedicated to delivering real impact on the climate and biodiversity crises through innovative projects of scale. Its aims are to create, restore, regenerate and rehabilitate biodiverse habitats across Ireland, to manage those habitats for ecological and recreational value in perpetuity and, in doing so, to maximise the ecosystem services they provide to people for the benefit of everyone, now and into the future. www.coillte.ie/coillte-nature

# Introduction

Its early morning and I set off with my dog Molly to walk to a woodland that is just five minutes from our house. On the way, we walk beneath a line of centuries-old oak trees that must have witnessed some interesting people passing by over the years on this quiet road to the village.

This land on all sides was once part of a large estate known as Glanmore, acquired in stages by one Francis Synge in the early nineteenth century. This was just a few years after the upheavals of the 1798 Rebellion and local people were still coming to terms with some horrific deaths in their own county. Some survivors were forced to take refuge in the local woods.[1] The tenants here were pleased that their new landlord was living locally in a big house at the edge of the Devil's Glen wood. Up to then, their rents had been paid to a land agent who worked for an absentee landlord.

To plan the expansion of his estate, Synge commissioned an extensive survey of the lands in this valley. In the eight years after 1816, he supervised the planting of over 160,000 trees on his newly acquired lands. I suspect that these included the oak trees that still line the road today. By 1840 there was also a group of small cottages, probably with thatched roofs, along the road between the young oak trees.

Ned Byrne's father had inherited the lease of twenty acres of good land here, including a small woodland, in the bottom of the valley. The laneway which led down to the river in the wood was used by all the occupants of the cottages to collect water for the houses and firewood for the hearths. In a corner of a field I find a heap of large stones, all that remains of the cottage that had been built by Ned's grandfather. It was in this cottage that Ned was born.

This was a time of serious difficulty for the Glanmore Estate. Francis Synge had died in 1831 and his son John Synge took over the running of the estate. But his tenants became increasingly impoverished and most lived on a diet dominated by potatoes. Some were evicted when they could not pay the rents. Meanwhile, the new landlord was spending money that he did not have to create a grand demesne and maintain his standing in society. He ignored the fact that the estate was falling deeper and deeper into debt. When he died in 1845, the very year that the Great Famine began, the estate was bankrupt and his son, called Francis Synge after his grandfather, was faced with court proceedings to sell the land and pay the debtors. But he managed, after several years, to buy back the estate house and some other properties.[2] Francis Synge was popular in the locality as he was said to be a hardworking farmer and looked after his tenants.

Ned was just a small child when the Potato Famine hit this area in 1846 but he could remember some of his neighbours being evicted and living in animal sheds through the winter. As a small child, he saw poor families make their last journey along the road beneath the growing oak trees. In the following years, many local people emigrated or tried to rebuild their lives. But Ned's parents were determined to stay and make the best of the situation, so he grew up working on his father's farm. In time this would be

Ned's farm and he loved the place. The work made him healthy and strong, just like the oak trees along the road whose canopies now gave passers-by some welcome shade from the summer sun.

As I walk along the same road, I search the ground beneath the trees for any new acorns that have fallen from the oak trees in the night or stare up into the vast tumble of branches and twigs, never failing to marvel at the sheer size and strength of these gentle giants. A cool wind blows down the valley from the mountain, sweeping across the fields and bending the branches of the trees. I watch the old hedge across the top field for a fox that I know lives just beyond it and for the rabbits that help her to survive through the year. Climbing the stile, I drop down the golden, bracken-covered slope and enter the shelter of the trees. A familiar hawthorn covered with red berries greets me as I pass beneath the mature ash and alder trees. I stand for a minute on the path to listen to the trickling water that flows down the hill from the line of groundwater springs. The air is cool and still on my face. A woodpecker's distinctive 'pick-pick' call and the ticking of a robin are the only evidence of birds in the dawn.

I walk over to my favourite tree, the biggest birch in the wood, and sit beneath it for a few minutes to absorb its wisdom and strength. The trunk is strengthened by splayed buttress roots just like the supports of a cathedral wall. High above, the branches spread wide with their spiral structure adding strength to the timber. This tree, which Ned probably climbed as a child, is now quite rotten in the centre. I can put my entire arm into a large cavity which once held the heartwood but the outer layers, or sapwood, of the tree are as vigorous as the day it was a young sapling in a new woodland.

For years, my own family had been searching for some land to establish a smallholding where we could grow our own food and cut wood for fuel, moving our lives more towards self-sufficiency with a lower environmental footprint. We had searched far and wide and, when Ned's farm was finally put on the market, we knew that it was again offering an opportunity. On the south-facing side of the valley were the permanent pasture fields and hedgerows where he had toiled all those years ago. I imagined him in summer driving the horse-drawn mower through the flower-rich meadow to save the hay that would sustain his cows over winter. The woodland where he and his sons had cut timber to roof the cow byre was still there in the valley and the river that wound its way down from the hills still flowed crystal clear.

Throwing caution to the wind, I cashed in part of my pension and bought the land outright. Even if times turned harder, I foolishly reckoned that I could sell the land and the timber to recover my investment. Instead, I fell in love with the place and began to spend more and more time there, experiencing all its moods and seasons, discovering its wildlife secrets and learning how to manage it properly. I realise now that our woodland has found its way into my heart.

For most of my adult life, I have worked to protect the environment – as a nature reserve warden, as director of a voluntary conservation body and more recently advising organisations, large and small, how to avoid or reduce damage to nature. Yet, during my lifetime, Ireland's wildlife has undergone a catastrophic decline. A third of all species groups examined in Ireland, including plants, birds, butterflies, freshwater fish and dragonflies, are either threatened with extinction or near-threatened. Birds that were once commonplace in the Irish countryside – the curlew, corncrake and yellow-hammer – have become so rare that it is a privilege to see even one. Water quality in our rivers and lakes has declined steadily so that now there are only a handful of 'pristine' inland waters. Ninety per cent of our highest-value habitats, listed under the EU's Habitats Directive, are in 'poor' or 'inadequate' condition. Ireland still has the lowest forest cover of any country in the European Union and little over one per cent of the country is occupied by native woodland.

After years of writing, protesting and trying to influence nature policy, I could see no change in this depressing trend and I worried for the future of our natural world. I needed to be inspired again and I knew that nature could provide this inspiration if I could just see some positive result for my efforts. In this land I found a project, no matter how small, where I could make a real contribution to restoring the natural environment. The baton had been passed from Ned's family to me to protect this heritage for the coming generations, including my children and grand-children. Everyone has something to offer, even if it is just planting a few trees or saving a hedgerow from destruction.

This land had also stirred up childhood memories from the days when I played in the local fields and woodland near my family home. Nobody seemed to know who owned that particular woodland so all the local kids met there after school. We lit campfires, built treehouses and made dams across the river that ran through the wood. I imagined that I was an adventurer in a far-away land carving out a place in the wilderness. In an attempt to keep me and my brothers at home, my father built a primitive wooden house in an old tree in our garden. It was entered by a rope ladder that we could pull up through a trapdoor. Without knowing it, I was re-enacting the type of lifestyle that my ancestors may have lived thousands of years ago.

Living close to nature is no longer a necessity today but more of a privilege. Centuries ago, it was the only option for most people as the growing human population scraped a living from the surface of the earth. But somewhere along the way we have lost that vital connection with nature. No longer do most people in the Western world have to build their own shelters, grow their staple food or catch their own dinner. This disconnect with the natural world has enormous implications for the protection of nature, but also for our personal happiness. Few modern children know the simple pleasures of climbing a tree, fishing in a stream or picking a handful of wild berries. Increasingly, we experience the natural world remotely – if at all – through television, the internet or through a car window.

Children today would have to search quite hard to find a woodland near their home. The native forests that once covered the island were cut and cleared centuries ago, leaving a country dominated by agriculture. While the colonial power that ruled Ireland for over 800 years is widely blamed for deforesting the country, most of the native woodland was already gone by the medieval period. By the early twentieth century, when Ireland achieved independence, there were just a few fragments of the old woodland remaining, a tiny fraction of which is classed as 'ancient woodland'. And, as the new country geared up to the modern world, it chose to replace the natural vegetation with fast-growing forests comprising exotic conifer species imported from North America. For most people today, a walk in the woods means visiting lines of dense, coniferous plantation or watching these forests cleared like a field of corn.

In the twenty-first century, Ireland's native woodland is in the emergency ward. A few of the remaining fragments are protected as nature reserves. Even there, uncontrolled deer populations are grazing out new seedlings and natural regeneration is rare. Invasive plants such as rhododendron and laurel infest many old estate woodlands blocking out the light and leaving the ground beneath bare and lifeless. Of the 1,320 sites covered in the National Survey of Native Woodland, 'the majority were small or very small in extent with half being six hectares or less and only three per cent of those surveyed being over 50 hectares'.[3] Traditional skills of woodland management, such as coppicing with standards, which can open dense canopies to let in the sunlight, have been largely forgotten. The patient is on life support and, unless radical treatment is administered, our grandchildren will not have a chance to experience the joy of the wild woods.

Becoming the owner of this farm and woodland was a special privilege for me but also a big responsibility. I had to learn to manage it properly. It all seemed a bit like a dream but my voyage of discovery had begun. Exploring this small piece of countryside is exciting. Finding old trees, looking for good places to cross a stream or just standing still to listen to the sounds in the wood is like experiencing childhood again. Simple pleasures for all the senses. I search for fallen nuts, collect sticks for the fire in winter or shoulder a fallen log, just as Ned would have done, and carry it back along the track to the house.

Everything in the world seems to be changing rapidly. Attitudes to the current climate breakdown are changing too and there is a growing awareness that planting trees and restoration of permanent woodland cover are among the best ways to capture the excess carbon that we are daily releasing to the atmosphere. But woodlands offer so much more – to our environment, to our health and as a renewable resource to replace the fossil fuels that will soon be in short supply.

Restoring Ireland's native woodland is just as important to me as safeguarding our traditional culture. Ned's farm and woodland are part of our heritage and should be passed on to future generations intact. But protection of this priceless asset will not happen by itself. It will take vision, commitment and long-term management such as that shown by some landowners in past centuries who planted trees for their grand-children and harvested timber that their grandparents had planted for them. The remaining native woods of Ireland are like fragments of a long-lost landscape.

They are disappearing and new native woodlands are not being added quickly enough to replace them. It is the equivalent of a decaying oak tree that is no longer producing seed. My ambition is to keep this one small patch of wildwood alive.

In this land, I had found the practical project and the inspiration that I needed. It offered no material profit but an opportunity to learn and to make a real difference to one small patch of wild nature. This book is the story of my journey of discovery about woodland here and in different parts of Ireland where other people are striving to hold on to these fragments of our heritage. Ned had a vision for the future of his land and it is our responsibility to make this happen.

## *Winter – Sleeping trees*

The oak trees were bare in the winter of 1860 when Ned's father, a previous tenant of our land, died suddenly in his late thirties having contracted pneumonia during a bout of severe weather. Ned was still a young man when he took over the tenancy of the farm from his father. The work was hard, but Ned was helped in the daily tasks by his teenage brothers. A few years later, his mother married a second time and moved out of the family home with the younger children to live with her new husband in the neighbouring townland. Ned married a local girl, Sarah, when he was twenty-five and she was just twenty. His new wife moved into the cottage and their first child, William, was born in the mild winter of 1869.

Fortunately, the weather was favourable in those years and things went well for the young family. Winters were less severe than those of Ned's father's time on the farm and they were able to cook and to heat the small cabin with firewood cut from the wood down by the river. The land was mainly tilled but by winter the family had harvested their potatoes and oats and the summer's hay was stacked in the yard. As well as the cows, they kept a few pigs which were allowed to roam in the woodland foraging for roots and bulbs. For Christmas, Ned killed one of the fattest and they ate well that year.

In December the sun rises late but I like to go out at first light or even before, while all the local people are still sleeping, as this is when the wildlife is most active. At this time of day, I see foxes, deer, buzzards and woodpeckers, all busy finding their first meal of the day, having survived another cold night. There is little or no disturbance, traffic noise is intermittent and natural sounds dominate.

It has been snowing for two days now with bitterly cold temperatures, enough to freeze the water in the puddles along the lane. There is a thick blanket of snow lying on the meadow where Ned once worked a century and a half before. The meadow was mowed last September and is still waiting for the spring signals to start growing again. I follow the tracks of a fox, weaving across the field, yet with a definite purpose. He detoured several times to investigate rabbit burrows and maybe a mouse beneath the grass. Winter is a tough time for our mammals when survival is the name of the game. Food is scarce and they must live on the fat they have accumulated during the summer. The bountiful days of autumn are gone and the last of the blackberries and sloes are now just a memory.

It is just after dawn and I am standing at the top of the field when an adult fox comes trotting along the hedge at the bottom. He is carrying some prey that looks like a small bird. Crossing the meadow, he slips effortlessly through a sheep fence in the corner and I watch him pick his way through some willow trees and into the woodland. I follow his trail which leads down a muddy track. Here there are lots of fox prints, droppings, feathers and scraps of bone that suggest many meals. In a corner beneath some brambles, I find the entrance to the fox earth. It is dark and secret. I doubt if many people have been here so the fox and his mate are mostly left to their own devices. As the sun rises over the valley, the lonely call of a soaring buzzard is the loudest sound.

I leave the fox in peace and enter a magical world of tall trees, flowing streams and ferns. In some places where the water bubbles to the surface, I sink to the top of my boots in soft, sucking mud. All around are small diggings where some other animal has been searching for buried food during the night. And then I come upon the badger sett. It is the largest and most active sett I have ever seen. Great mounds of spoil lie outside the entrances to a maze of underground tunnels and regular trails lead off in several directions into the undergrowth.

The trees around the badger sett are tall and their trunks close together, with many even entwined as if they are closely connected below ground. I can identify nearly a dozen types of trees all mixed together in seemingly random order. There are standing dead stems, known to foresters as snags, and there is plenty of fallen timber in various states of decay. In places, I have to wade through shallow water to pass by a dense jungle of bramble, fern and honeysuckle.

Some of the older hazel and alder trees have huge bases and multiple stems, suggesting that these were cut a century and a half ago by Ned and his family to produce a continuous crop of timber that had many uses on the farm. In those days, horses would have been used to extract heavy timbers. I can imagine the men working together as a team among the trees. Since those days the woodland has been largely forgotten by the local farmers as the ground is too wet for cultivation and livestock are discouraged from entering here for fear that they will become trapped in the soft ground.

### Getting to know the wood

I spent the first year after becoming the owner of Ned's Wood just observing and getting to know my way around the place. Finding a dry path was important as some areas flood in the winter and it is good to be able to keep dry feet. This meant building a boardwalk across some small springs and streams. As well as the fox, I found where the tracks of deer and badgers were leading in and out of the wood. I found many fallen trees, some recent but others so rotten that they had almost been absorbed back into the woodland soil. I found the best areas for bluebells and wild garlic and I made a note of the locations of old hazel trees that might provide a good source of poles later on.

Ned's Wood lies in a fold of the Wicklow landscape that makes it difficult to see from anywhere, even from the top of nearby Carrick Mountain. Close by is a well-known landmark, the Devil's Glen, where the River Vartry flows through a deep glacial gorge filled with a mixed woodland. One small tributary of this river rises to the west and powers down through a wide valley carrying leaves and sticks from many small copses and plantations along its banks. The woodland itself is small, about three hectares, and it has grown up in the wet floodplain of the river, where the water frequently overtops its banks and spreads out to saturate the soils. This makes parts of it impassable in winter.

The woodland is dominated by tall trees reaching towards the light. Unlike a planted forest, this native woodland has a tangled mixture of species, ages and sizes of tree that has evolved over centuries. The trunks are fairly close together and in summer the canopy is dense, casting a deep shadow on the ground below. The commonest trees are alder but there is plenty of ash, birch, holly, hazel and oak with willow in more open areas. In winter, when the leaves have gone, the alder trees still hold onto their crop of tiny cones, the seed from which has long blown away in the wind. Alder is adapted to living in waterlogged soils and the largest specimens grow along the riverbank where their roots are permanently in the water.

Alder has a close relationship with a specialised bacterium, *Frankia alni*, in its roots. The bacteria absorb nitrogen from the air and make it available to the tree. In return, the alder tree provides the bacteria with sugars and minerals, and they use these to create enzymes which are eventually converted into amino acids – the building blocks of protein. When the leaves fall, they also add mulch and more nitrogen to the soil as well as providing food for worms and other decomposers. This nitrogen then becomes available to other trees in the wood. I have often found holly growing so close to an alder tree that it looks like it is in an embrace. The holly clearly benefits from the nitrogen levels in the soil around its neighbour. When a branch falls, the exposed wood of the alder is a rich orangey-red colour, but the timber is light and does not make good firewood due to its high moisture content.

The fact that alder evolved to grow best in wet soils made it a valuable wood for many specialised uses over the centuries. A fast-growing hardwood, it was widely used for building boats, mill wheels and

anything that was frequently in contact with water.⁴
During the Industrial Revolution, alder was used to
make wooden clogs for the workers who had to stand
all day on the cold, wet floors of the factories, mills
and mines of England. When Ned was a child in the
mid-nineteenth century, he would have seen men from
Lancashire making clogs in the woods around this part
of Wicklow. These migrant woodsmen lived among the
trees where they worked and the local children called
them the 'cloggers'.

After one year, the wood started to feel familiar. I
knew when to expect the first leaves on each of the trees
and where the deer liked to wallow in a muddy hollow.
But I am just a casual visitor to the wood compared
with indigenous forest dwellers around the world, who
know every corner of their habitat as well as I know my
own house.

### History in the woodland

In the early days of exploring the woodland, I began
to get curious about its history. How old are the trees?
Were they planted or did they seed themselves? Were
they ever cut down or managed? Did anyone ever live
here?

My first sources of information were old maps. In the nineteenth century, the Ordnance Survey of Ireland was run by the British military authorities. Army sappers and their officers were dispatched to the far corners of the empire with their draftsmen and chain measures. Invented by the English mathematician Edmund Gunter in the early seventeenth century, the chain used by the soldiers measured exactly twenty-two yards (about twenty metres) long and was divided into one hundred links. I pity the men who had to carry this around!

Few local place names had been written down before this, so the soldiers talked to local people and interpreted the Irish names as best they could. There were often puzzling results. The Irish word for woodland, *coill*, was sometimes confused with *cill*, meaning church, so the wooded origin of a townland might be forgotten. But they did produce the first accurate maps of the countryside which were published at a scale of six inches to one mile.

By the 1830s, so-called 'old stand woodland' had been reduced to only a fifth of one per cent of the land area of Ireland when the British Army surveyors scoured the Irish landscape for the first edition of the six-inch scale maps. In Britain, ancient woodland survived for much longer but it is estimated that more than a third of that remaining there was destroyed in the second half of the twentieth century as modern agriculture was rolled out.[5]

On the 1834 map sheet for this part of Wicklow I found the river which forms the boundary of our small townland. Sure enough, it shows a line of large trees along the banks just in the location where some giant alder trees stand today. By the 1920s, and the last edition of the Ordnance Survey six-inch maps, the outline of Ned's Wood was much as it remains today. The line of cottages along the road had gone, leaving only the vague outline of stones in the field and fading memories of the tenant families that lived there. Perhaps the dwindling population in the area meant less pressure for firewood and other timber, which allowed trees to grow to maturity. Old maps and documents give us an insight into how the land would have looked but they only go back a century or two. To understand the origins of woodland in the wider countryside, I need to go back a lot longer.

### Does wildwood survive today?

The early clearance of the natural forests in Ireland suggests that virtually everything we see today is secondary growth. However, there could be sites where ancient woodland persists in places that have a history of forest cover. Oliver Rackham of Cambridge University made an exhaustive search of Ireland for any fragments of ancient woodland that may have remained. He used a number of clues to recognise such areas.[6]

Place names such as Derry (*doire* or oakwood) or Youghal (*eochaill* or yewwood) suggest not only that the site was wooded but indicate the dominant tree species. However, on most such sites there is no trace of remaining woodland. A few exceptions include Derrycunihy wood in Killarney, which is still an oak-wood today. Old documentation such as *The Civil Survey of Ireland in 1654–56* gives details of thousands of woods by townland. Analysing these extensive records, Rackham estimated that Ireland had at least 170,000 hectares of woodland in the mid-seventeenth century covering over two per cent of the land area. He considered that, by comparison with contemporary English woodlands, the Irish woodlands were in a neglected state by this stage.

After the Cromwellian conquest of Ireland, large tracts of land were transferred to former soldiers to reward them for their loyalty. The Civil Survey, based as it was on the records of the original owners and not the result of an official or government survey, was considered by many of the new owners to be inaccurate. The Down Survey (so-called because a chain was laid *down* and a scale made) was organised from 1656 to 1658 under the direction of William Petty. The survey employed about a thousand men, mostly unemployed soldiers, and was carried out very rapidly. Using the Civil Survey as a guide, teams of surveyors were sent out under Petty's direction to measure every townland to be forfeited to soldiers and adventurers. The resulting maps, made at a scale of forty perches to one inch, were the first systematic mapping of a large area on such a scale attempted anywhere. The primary purpose of these maps was to record the boundaries of each townland and to calculate their areas with great precision. The maps are also rich in other detail showing churches, roads, rivers, castles, houses and fortifications, and also include some woodlands. When his mapping was finished, Petty had difficulty in collecting some of the agreed payments. To settle this debt, nearly 10,000 acres of land were trans-ferred to him, but he was not out of the woods yet. He was charged with fraud as the allocations of land to him in lieu of payment were alleged to be over-stated.

I checked Petty's map for this part of Wicklow to see if there were any tree symbols on our land. Strangely, there is a large unshaded area covering this townland with the word 'unforfeited' printed across it in handwritten script. This must mean that it was retained in the original ownership. So, it gives me no further clues to the ancient history of our woodland.

Signs of historical woodland industries are another indicator of antiquity. Walking across the hill in the Devil's Glen, another old woodland site close to my home, I have sometimes come across a circular platform about the size of a small garden. Scooping away the deep leaf mould from centuries of leaf-fall, I find a debris of charred wood in the soil indicating that this forest was once used for the industrial process of charcoal-making.

Good charcoal is mostly pure carbon, called *char*. This was made by 'cooking' wood for a long period in a low-oxygen environment, a process that could take days and burned off volatile compounds such as water, methane, hydrogen and tar. The process leaves black lumps and powder, about one-quarter of the original weight. When set alight, the carbon in charcoal combines with oxygen and forms carbon dioxide, carbon monoxide, water, other gases releasing significant quantities of energy. Because charcoal burns hotter, cleaner and more evenly than wood, it was used by smelters for melting iron ore in blast furnaces, and by blacksmiths who formed and shaped iron tools. Commercial production was first done in pits covered with soil by specially trained craftsmen called colliers. Charcoal-making was widespread in the country up to the eighteenth century. Isaac Weld wrote in 1807 of the Killarney woods:

> Not long since all these mountains were clothed down to the water's edge with oaks of large growth; most of these venerable trees have fallen to the axe which has been busily plied year after year. The destruction of these forests is principally attributable to the manufacture of iron – a business carried on with great spirit in various parts of the country and for which an abundant supply of charcoal was required. As fuel became scarce, the iron works declined, and at last they were totally abandoned. The woods are now cut for other purposes, as timber in this country is becoming extremely valuable, in consequence of the prodigal use that was formerly made of it.[7]

Among the indicators of very old woodland is the presence of certain trees such as the whitebeam and crab apple. Yew trees are another indicator of ancient pedigree, but yew woods are now very rare and of special interest. The Killarney yew wood is one of the oldest known stands in Europe and is estimated to be over 3000 years old.[8] The yews themselves are gnarled and twisted. They bear bright scarlet fruits in autumn – a delicacy for thrushes and blackbirds.

Oliver Rackham of Cambridge University also suggested that lichens or Atlantic mosses and liverworts could be used as indicators of antiquity. Using a combination of all these clues, he concluded that much less ancient woodland survived in Ireland because of the depredations of a burgeoning population in the centuries leading up to the Great Famine of the 1840s.

Frazer Mitchell, of Trinity College Dublin, has confirmed from pollen analysis that Irish forests have been in constant flux over the last 10,000 years and that periods of stability were rare and short-lived. The interplay of a constantly changing climate and evolving human impacts on the landscape made for a dynamic history in the woods. The concept of a stable forest being undisturbed for thousands of years is not

supported by the available evidence. Conservation
management of the remaining native woodland needs
to accept this history of dynamic change and to be
aware of the sensitivity of the forests to minor changes
in future climate.[9]

## Coppicing

As February hands over the baton to March there are
signs that winter is coming to a close. I am convinced
that the shade cast later in the year by a dense canopy
in some of our wood is restricting the ground flora and
preventing regeneration of trees. The darkest areas are
beneath the large holly trees that grow in the dryer soils
near the bank of the river. The ground is covered in little
more than some creeping ivy and slowly decaying holly
leaves that have dropped from the trees. At the south of
the wood there are a number of old hazel trees that are
so shaded they produce few flowers in the spring and
hardly any hazelnuts in autumn. So, there is no regeneration of hazel. It is time to introduce some positive
management here.

Fortunately, my friend Mike Carswell, an experienced woodsman, lives and carries on his craft in
Wicklow. I spend a while with Mike working out what

we are going to do to encourage regrowth in the hazel area. Finally, we decide that the only way to bring sunlight back to this dark place is to cut some of the holly trees to the ground and coppice the hazels. So, the work begins with the help of various volunteers.

Mature holly produces fine timber that is hard and dense with narrow growth rings. We cut the trunks into pieces about two metres long and stack them high to season in the woodland. Next to receive attention are the old hazel trees. Mike cuts the multiple stems back to the stump (or stool) as close as possible to ground level as there is evidence that these have been cut in the past. Using traditional tools, such as the billhook and slasher, he clears brambles and other vegetation from around the trunks before felling begins. A number of the hazel stems are cut most of the way through but a thin sliver of connection to the root system is retained. Then he bends the long stems out from the centre and weighs them down to the ground with heavy stones. Beneath the stones he has scraped the bark off the hazel branches to encourage rooting. The result is a strange structure with long branches spread out like spider's legs from the body of the stool in the centre. The branches still gain sustenance from the established roots of the tree but almost immediately start to develop new root systems beneath the stones. In a few years I will be able to sever the umbilical connections and we will have a small coppice of new hazel trees.

The term 'coppice' is derived from the French verb *couper*, meaning to cut. Coppicing is the oldest known form of woodland management and would have been employed to provide the hazel wattle fences used to make fish traps in Dublin Bay in the Mesolithic period.[10] By cutting broadleaf trees during their dormant winter phase, the trees do not die but send up vibrant new shoots which grow on to become poles. Each time these are harvested, the trees re-shoot and a sustainable harvest of timber is collected. The coppicing process also allows light into the woodland floor which stimulates the growth of flowering plants and natural regeneration of trees. Theoretically, a coppiced tree can live indefinitely as the stools continually produce new wood. A wood managed in this way traditionally contains coppiced trees, or underwood, and scattered tall trees known as standards. Within a single coppiced wood, some of the underwood is normally cut in winter, resulting in a patchwork of *coupes* at different stages of growth. Among the native trees which readily coppice are alder, ash, birch, hazel, oak, sycamore and willow. The interval between cropping depends on the species and the intended product. Hazel is usually cut every seven to ten years while ash and oak are generally harvested after twenty-five to thirty years of growth.

Many people visiting a woodland may be unaware that it was intensively managed by coppicing in previous centuries. It seems that many of the surviving oak woods in this country were managed in the past as 'coppice with standards'. In the Glen of the Downs, County Wicklow, there is a path bisecting the woodland. On one side of this path is the classic sign of coppicing: stools of oak up to two metres across, while a uniform stand of timber oaks occurs on the other side. This would suggest that the latter area was clear-felled at some stage and later regenerated or was replanted with a single-age stand of trees.

Mike and I have visited a number of old woodlands in Wicklow and we have found evidence of coppicing, such as large stools with multiple stems, in many of these. Another small example is Woodbank near Lough Dan where almost all of the oaks have multiple stems. We have found similar evidence in our woodland, which was coppiced by Ned and his sons in the late nineteenth century. He probably learnt this technique from the estate woodsmen who worked in the surrounding forests.

Coppicing was already a well-established practice in the Neolithic period when buildings were constructed with oak for the structural elements and walls made with hazel wattle and daub. Other species that may have been used in the wattle screens included alder, ash and birch.[11] This was still the main construction method in the Viking period based on the large number of houses that have been excavated in the centre of Dublin.

Matthew Jebb, director of the National Botanic Gardens, has demonstrated that the renewable timber for a single Viking house could have been harvested from a tenth of a hectare of well-managed coppice, with reeds for thatching the roof, all from the surrounding countryside. The natural decay of these materials coincided with the 15- to 20-year regrowth period of the coppice. In theory, Medieval Dublin's 900-odd houses could therefore have been sustained in perpetuity from a mere 100 hectares of such woodland – or about half the size of the modern Dublin Port. While all of these materials were quite easily damaged by fire, they were easily replaced and all housing was then completely sustainable.

The Brehon Laws from the eighth century AD outline the standards of the time for woodland maintenance. Hazel laths and woven hawthorn hedges were to be planted on raised banks around valuable hazel coppices to protect them from grazing animals. These coppices produced essential construction material, bark, nuts, fruit and tree masts, but were also used for beehives and honey production.[12]

The best documented information on coppicing is from the eighteenth century. Samuel Hayes, a member of the Irish parliament and a large landowner in County Wicklow, wrote a remarkable *Treatise on Planting and the Management of Woods and Coppices* in 1794.[13] His seemingly endless sentences and strange language make this a struggle to read. However, his work is essentially a handbook on native woodland management as observed on his own estate at Avondale, near Rathdrum. He wrote,

A considerable profit may thus be made of our plantations or coppice woods, even of a very few years growth, and both may in time be converted into open groves, where the branching heads of well grown healthy trees, at thirty feet asunder,

shall afford more shade and shelter, than ten times
their number, suffered to crowd each other, in the
ordinary method of management.

This shows that, over two centuries ago, Hayes was
promoting the sustainable management of woodlands
in his ownership and he gives a lot of space in his book
to the monetary value of such woods.

The historical practice of coppicing in Wicklow was
also researched by the forester Michael Carey in his
book *If Trees Could Talk*.[14] He relied heavily on the
woodland surveys of the Coolattin estate over a forty-
year period in the mid-eighteenth century. In this estate,
the total area of coppiced woodlands, or springwoods
as they were generally referred to in the surveys, was
as high as 500 hectares, mainly in the south of the
county. The management system used here was based
on that devised in south Yorkshire, the home base
of the Marquis of Rockingham. Coppice products in
eighteenth- and nineteenth-century Ireland included
bark for tanning, charcoal for smelting iron, building
materials, timber for fencing, gates and furniture,
handles for multiple farm tools and ploughs, stakes for
planting new trees, shingles for roofs and even heels for

ladies' shoes. Barrel staves were also very commonly made to export fish and other perishables from Arklow port to England. Any of the odd-shaped pieces and offcuts went into the charcoal burner or the woodstack to be dried for winter fuel.

In the late eighteenth century, the Dublin Society (now the RDS) became a promoter of woodland management giving grants to landowners for fencing and planting of coppices. Despite these efforts, the production of coppiced timber became uneconomic in the nineteenth century and many intensively managed woods were allowed to grow into high forest, inter-planted with conifers or cleared altogether to make way for more farmland. This is why, when we walk in the few remaining native woodlands today, we find ample evidence of former coppicing and a way of life that is all but forgotten in Ireland.

### Managing a wildwood

In a few places, coppicing has been revived as a form of nature conservation management. St John's Wood in County Roscommon is recognised as one of the few ancient woodlands surviving in the midlands. Close by are the ruins of a medieval town called Rindoon (in

Irish this means fort on the promontory). From 1227
to 1340, this was a Norman town with a population
of at least a thousand people although it had probably
been a site of human settlement for centuries before that.
Just over a kilometre away on the same peninsula is St
John's Wood. This was probably a source of building
materials, firewood and other wood products for the
Rindoon settlement.

This woodland is mentioned in the Civil Survey
of 1656 and is shown on the Ordnance Survey maps
of 1837 in exactly the same location where it survives
today. The woodland is dominated by oak and hazel
but with a mix of ash, holly, rowan and wych elm in
the canopy. This former coppice with standards has
massive oak stools, up to three and a half metres across,
and was last managed in this way as recently as the
1920s. Oliver Rackham, who has written extensively
on woodland history in Britain and Ireland, found at
least twenty-five species of shrubs and trees in St John's
Wood which is much more than other, younger sites.
With an extensive cover of mosses and liverworts, he
considered these woodlands to be coppiced versions of
a rainforest. Unfortunately, almost all of the oldest trees
in the woodland were felled after a change of ownership

in 1917. The oldest surviving tree, a pollarded pedunculate oak of almost three and a half metres in girth, was estimated to be at least 150–200 years old. This land was acquired by the state through the Land Commission in a series of plots over many years, but some of the woodland remains in private ownership.

Not surprisingly for a habitat that has been under forest cover for a very long time, St John's Wood is also rich in insects and other small creatures. A survey in 2010 identified a total of 823 invertebrate species in a rich and varied assemblage. Of particular importance are a number of small animals that depend on decaying wood with at least eighteen per cent of the Irish fauna in this one location. Both canopy invertebrates, including moths, beetles, bugs and spiders, and ground layer invertebrates are rich in species. The range of molluscs here is characteristic of pristine ancient woodland and includes three nationally threatened species. The butterflies, moths and two-winged flies are especially species-rich and include several species not previously identified in Ireland. Finally, those species that feed on fungi, especially fungus gnats, have a particularly high diversity.[15]

In the 2000s, there was a considerable amount of management work undertaken here including coppicing of hazel by experienced woodsman Joe Gowran, to open the canopy up to more sunlight and to produce rods for various crafts. A detailed ecological study of St John's Wood was undertaken in 2007 by Aidan Corcoran at UCD.[16] He worked with Joe Gowran and has a practical understanding of this traditional craft of coppicing. It was evident that coppicing had been carried out here in the past, but most of the hazel in the wood had not been cut for up to seventy years. Much of the previously coppiced hazel was derelict and unused. This is a common feature in woods where coppicing has ceased and the hazel trees may eventually die about seventy years after last being cut. Corcoran found that the structure of St John's Wood had been shaped by a long history of woodland management which had allowed open-habitat species to survive within the wood.

A stone wall bisects St John's Wood with the western side of this intended to be maintained as a reference area with no intervention. The coppicing management in the 2000s was carried out only on the eastern section of the woodland. All woody plants, except for mature trees (known as standards) were cut allowing light to penetrate to the woodland floor and encourage the ground flora to develop. However, this needs to be done on a rotational basis with various woodland *coupes*, or clearings, cut each year to allow the new growth of rods to develop from the cut stumps.

Managing a coppice with standards is a balancing act. The more standards are retained, the less light is available for coppice regrowth. In Corcoran's opinion 'regeneration of hazel in St John's Wood has been poor, chiefly as a consequence of the retention of too many standards'. His view is that five fully mature trees and ten to fifteen developing standards per hectare is the ideal target for 'coppice with standards' management.

Unfortunately, there has been inconsistency in the management measures. Joe Gowran says 'the cut biomass needs to be removed to get more benefit from the coppice cycle in relation to ground flora. Traditional coppice management requires more intervention, particularly on bramble control, than is presently being employed here.' Continuity of management is needed in these rich woodland habitats to ensure the highest biodiversity is maintained.

On my last visit to St John's Wood, I walked through the trees one evening and crept down through closely spaced stems of the hazel cut by Gowran to the waters of Lough Ree. Mosses and lichens clothed the trees and there was a humid feel to the air. Although the only sound was the lapping of lake waters, I could imagine the wood filled with the noises of medieval woodsmen, felling trees by hand axe and chatting as they worked.

## Badger watching

It is cold and still as I walk across our meadow in the fading light and I can feel the hint of a frost forming on the grass. I climb the stile that I made in the sheep fence and enter the wood, trying not to get snagged on last season's brambles. Following the familiar outlines of the trees I find the one I am looking for, a substantial tree with one limb lying prostrate on the ground where it has fallen in some past storm but has continued to grow. I scramble into its lower branches using a rope that I leave here as a climbing aid and look down at the badger sett which dominates the hillside below me.

There has been a lot of recent digging here which resembles the work of a small bulldozer. The soft earth and stones have been cleaned out of some dark holes in the slope where there are wide trails that look like the slides in a children's playground. Occasional piles of dead grass and bracken indicate that the occupants have been cleaning out their winter bedding in readiness for the birth of cubs. The huge mounds of earth outside the entrances suggest that there is an extensive system of tunnels and chambers in there. The ground beneath the tree is criss-crossed by well-worn tracks through the vegetation. I settle into a familiar crook between three branches and wait for the darkness to come as a light breeze blows from the sett towards me.

It is dark now as I stare towards a large hole in the ground below me. I think I see something moving in the entrance, or is it just my imagination? There it is again, a definite face with broad black and white stripes, actively sniffing the passing air. Unsurprisingly, for an animal that lives underground for most of its life, badgers have quite poor eyesight and rely mainly on their stronger senses of smell and hearing. I pull the hood down across my face and sit as still as I can. Slowly, cautiously, the large animal emerges from the burrow and, finally satisfied that there are no unusual smells or sounds, he starts a vigorous bout of scratching. It has been a long day sleeping in an underground chamber and it is good to get out in the air.

Before long, another face appears at the sett entrance and a second animal emerges. With little ceremony that resembles foreplay, the larger animal smells the tail of the smaller female and then mounts her briefly making her squeal and squirm to escape. The female is clearly in oestrus, which suggests that she has already given birth to cubs and is now receptive again. Badgers mate a year ahead of the next birth, but the pregnancy is delayed by a process known as delayed implantation. The fertilised eggs remain unattached in the uterus in a state of suspended development until they implant in the tissue of the wall and begin to develop a foetus in the following December. This remarkable phenomenon, unknown in humans, allows the animals maximum opportunities for mating while ensuring that the cubs are born the following spring when there is plenty of forage available.[17]

Badgers are common and widespread in Ireland despite the culling undertaken by the Department of Agriculture in a misguided attempt to reduce the prevalence of bovine tuberculosis by exterminating wild carriers of the disease. The last national survey in the Republic of Ireland in the 1990s estimated that there could be up to a quarter of a million badgers in the country organised into 50,000 social groups of related animals.[18] In Northern Ireland, some 33,500 badgers in 7,500 social groups, were estimated in a 2007–08 survey.[19]

I had several approaches by agriculture officials who wanted to cull the badgers on our land but I refused to allow this to happen and, instead, mounted an automatic sensor camera opposite the sett entrances. Now, new research shows that badgers start to roam much further afield when culling starts nearby, potentially *increasing* the spread of bovine tuberculosis, the disease that culling is meant to control. Surviving badgers in populations that are culled cover nearly two-thirds more land each month than they did before the culling began, and the likelihood of a badger visiting neighbouring territories each night increases twentyfold, according to a study from the Institute of Zoology in London. The increase in the badgers' range comes despite most of the animals less frequently leaving their setts in the aftermath of a cull.[20]

Happily, our sett has not been disturbed so far and the camera has recorded some other interesting images that I was not expecting. Two small cubs emerged cautiously later in the spring and played around at the sett entrance before following the adults on their foraging expeditions in the surrounding fields. An adult fox also seems to be living side by side with the badgers as one has been regularly around the sett entrances. Other mammals I photographed here were rabbit, wood mouse, pine marten and our own farm cat on one of his night-time hunting trips.

This has almost certainly been a main badger sett for centuries as there are huge spoil heaps outside the ten or so entrances. I am sure Ned was aware of it as he mowed the meadow above a century ago. I estimate that the tunnels must go for tens of metres into the hillside and there may even be breeding chambers under our vegetable garden. I can imagine a badger in its tunnel, nibbling the bottom off some of our carrots.

While badgers would catch and eat a baby rabbit, their main diet is made up of less mobile prey such as earthworms with up to 200 worms eaten in a single night.[21] Mild, moist nights are best for foraging when the worms are likely to be near or out on the surface of the soil. After a good scratch at the entrance to the sett, and careful sniffing of the air for any scent of a competitor, including a human, the badgers head off on their nightly foraging trips. I know that they cross the meadow because I have followed their tracks through the grass in the morning, noting the small holes that they have dug to find earthworms or cranefly larvae.

The Irish name for the badger is *broc*. The townland called Brockagh near Glendalough means a place of

badgers according to P.W. Joyce.²² He also points to
Brockabeg in the midlands; Brockish and Brockaghs
in Antrim; and Brockles, Brocklis, Brocklusk and
Brockless 'in various counties', so local people long ago
were certainly noticing these secretive animals. It was
said years ago that badgers – like black cats – can bring
bad luck or good luck. If the badger walked across the
path behind someone, they were in for very good luck.
However, if the badger walked across the path in front,
and if it happened to scrape up a bit of earth as it went,
then it was time to choose one's coffin! Country folk
once believed that badgers held funerals for their dead
kin. Sometimes, in fact, badgers die underground and
the chambers will be sealed. Years later, when soil and
old bedding are dug out, the bones go out too. I once
found a badger skull among fresh diggings outside a sett
which suggests that this was an exhumation.

My camera reveals that adult badgers are quite
rough with their cubs. They will grab them by the
ears and pull them around. Mating behaviour is not
a tender thing either. The male bites the female on the
neck before mounting her amid loud squeals and much
wrestling. Badgers are very strong and, when cornered,
an adult will fight tenaciously. This led to the cruel

'sport' of badger-baiting where the sett would be partly dug out with dogs and trapped badgers made fight to the death in a pit. Thankfully, this practice is now illegal but the persecution of the badger continues in a misguided attempt to control bovine TB in many parts of the country. I am determined that these permanent residents in our woodland will continue their quiet lives without disturbance.

### Invasive species

Our native trees, like the badger, are those that arrived in Ireland since the last Ice Age and have thus been in the country for thousands of years. By contrast, there are also many trees and shrubs that were introduced just centuries ago by landowners who planned to 'improve' their estates. Among these are beech, sweet chestnut and cotoneaster that have become naturalised and add to the variety in the landscape. Some of these introduced species are more aggressive and will invade new areas once released into the wild. Rhododendron and cherry laurel are probably the most invasive in woodland as they both can spread by seed and suckers and they also cast a dense shade preventing regeneration of the native species. Both species are hugely difficult to control.

Others, such as sycamore, produce a rain of seed every year that fills any spaces with a dense cluster of seedlings.

Winter is time to start removing the sycamore that has become established in places in our woodland. Although it can be a fine tree, sycamore is not native to Ireland having been introduced from central and southern Europe. Nobody is sure when it was brought to Ireland but it is now the second most common hedgerow tree in Ireland after the ash. I used to play in a sycamore tree when I was a child and I remember the sticky deposit on branches that is produced by aphids sucking juices from the leaves. In summer the flowers become winged seeds that we used to call helicopters as they spiral down to the ground in the autumn winds. In most years there is an abundant crop of seeds and these result in a prolific forest of seedlings that are quite shade tolerant. Given time, sycamore will replace other tree species, especially ash, in a woodland. The other characteristic of sycamore is that it can live quite well in salt winds and will be found thriving in harsh conditions such as those on offshore islands, sand dunes and the top of sea cliffs.

I have persuaded a friend, Mark Lewis, to use his climbing skills and professional training as a tree surgeon to take down the sycamores in two groups in the wood. Using the ropes and tackle that any serious rock climber would employ, he shins to the top like a squirrel and begins to lop off the upper branches. One by one he drops each branch to the ground under the tree until only a bare trunk remains. Then he hoists himself to the top again and takes off manageable sections into a neat pile on the ground. Some people are surprised that I have decided to remove these broad-leaved trees. However, it is not a tree that supports many other species. For example, only fifty insects and mites are known to live on sycamore while nearly 450 of these species inhabit the oaks in Britain and Ireland.

Luckily, sycamore and a single beech are the only non-native trees I have found so far in our woodland. Very few native woodlands in Ireland have avoided invasion by either rhododendron or laurel which are much more of a problem to deal with. *The National Survey of Native Woodlands* found that rhododendron occurred in nearly a quarter of all the woodlands surveyed and laurel in one-fifth. In around half of these sites, infestation levels were classified as high.[23] Rhododendron plants were first brought to Ireland by the Victorians to add to the ornamental collections in gardens and great estates where its attractive blossoms are like decorations against the shiny, dark green leaves. It was subsequently planted to provide shelter in many western seaboard locations. It is a large perennial evergreen, an acid-loving shrub that is native to the Iberian Peninsula and Asia. There are over 900 species of rhododendron, but only *Rhododendron ponticum* is invasive in Ireland. Since its introduction, rhododendron has escaped into the wild and is particularly invasive in the west, north-west and south-west of the country. It thrives in areas with mild, moist climatic conditions and can colonise a range of habitats including woodland, peatland, grassland, urban areas, roadsides and waste-lands. Luckily, it has not arrived in our wood yet.

Once established, it forms dense, long-lived thickets that smother the ground flora and suppress the regeneration of native trees and shrubs. Its dense thickets can reach several metres in height and eventually form a toxic layer of leaf litter which produces a dark sterile environment and supports little wildlife. The foliage of rhododendron is unpalatable to grazing animals. Dense tangles of rhododendron stems can smother watercourses and block pathways. Each flower head can produce over 5,000 seeds. This means that a single rhododendron bush can produce over a million seeds per year. Rhododendron seeds are amongst the smallest and lightest of any plant species and are designed primarily for dispersal by wind. They can be blown up to a hundred metres from the parent plant. It is also capable of reproducing by vegetative means, both by suckering from roots and by layering wherever branches touch the ground.

I have seen serious cases of rhododendron infestation in woodlands of the national parks at Killarney, Glenveagh, Connemara and the Wicklow Mountains. The thickets are often so dense that they become impenetrable and the deer populations avoid browsing the waxy leaves. By 1990, an estimated three-quarters of the 1,200 hectares of native woodland in Killarney National Park was infested with this highly invasive species and, in the management plan produced that year, the National Park managers set themselves the target of eradicating rhododendron from three-quarters of the woodland in the park within twenty years. After ten years it was estimated that approximately forty per cent of the infested oak woods had been cleared of the invasive species by park staff, contractors and the non-government organisation Groundwork. Every summer since 1981, hundreds of volunteers from many parts of the globe came to do the hard, physical work of tackling this problem.

In 2008, the National Parks and Wildlife Service (NPWS) published a guide to management of rhodo-dendron in nature conservation areas. As well as the tried-and-tested physical removal, this guide advocated herbicide treatment, brash management and spot spraying of saplings and seedlings.[24] These techniques were referred to in a new management plan for the National Park covering the period 2005 to 2009 but, in 2013, some thirty-two years after the clearance work began, the Groundwork team returned to survey the woodlands where the volunteers had worked. Of the three areas visited all were found to have flowering rhododendron which had resulted in thousands of seedlings recolonising the cleared areas.[25] This illustrates not only the difficulty of eradicating this vigorous alien plant but also the need for ongoing work to remove all seedlings and prevent regrowth.

I am glad that the only non-native tree I have to deal with is sycamore, but I can see seedlings of the now deceased parents everywhere in the wood where there is some sunlight. Weeding seedlings out by hand is a tedious job so I might take a strimmer to the denser plants.

## *Girdling trees*

Most of the mature sycamores in our wood can be removed by felling but there are several large trees that I definitely cannot fell as they grow on or close to the large badger sett in the wood. If I did fell these trees all in one go it would create so much disturbance, exposing the entrances to the weather, that the occupants would be sure to desert their traditional home. An alternative approach that I am using is called ring-barking or girdling the trees. This involves cutting one or two grooves in the bark and underlying cambium around the entire trunk near the base. This blocks the ducts which carry the water and nutrients up through the live sapwood to feed the branches and the tree will slowly die of thirst. It is harder labour than I thought as I have to work bent low on a steep slope and there are serious safety considerations when using a chainsaw in this situation.

When trees are girdled in the winter, they usually come into leaf the following spring. A vigorous species, such as sycamore, may produce leaves for two summers after ring-barking. Our trees have produced abundant seed each year, possibly as a natural response to attack. Two years later I have started to notice that the top branches of the sycamores I ring-barked are looking bare of leaves and that other branches have leaves that have gone prematurely brown in summer. As the trees slowly die, they first shed their leaves, then the smaller twigs and branches. Three years after girdling most trees have a stem that is sound and dry, ideal for firewood as it needs no further storage and can be taken straight from the woodland to the stove. Girdled broadleaved trees will fall to the ground because dead branches are less likely to get caught up on their neighbours. A typical girdled tree can remain standing for five years or more until root decay makes it topple. I am hoping that there will be a slow decay and disintegration of the sycamores so I have planted the area with young hazel trees that will grow quite rapidly and hopefully provide alternative cover for the badgers emerging on their nightly forays.

Fast-growing trees such as birch and alder stay wet when they die and soon start to degrade. These standing trees, or snags, are valuable habitats for wildlife if allowed to rot as they are colonised by wood-boring insects and bees, woodpeckers and other hole-nesting birds. Conventional felling produces sudden gaps in the canopy that increase the exposure of neighbouring trees to sun and wind. This sudden exposure can cause trees to stop growing. Oaks often produce epicormic shoots (side growth from the bark) after a thinning – this reduces the value of their timber although it would not be a problem in our woodland where I will be leaving any diseased trees to die a natural death. By contrast, girdling slowly opens gaps in the canopy over several years as the girdled tree dies, allowing the crowns of neighbouring trees to grow into the space provided. Condemning a mature tree to a slow death is not something I like doing but it is a management method that has the best interests of the badgers and the whole woodland at heart.

## Woodlands for health

Like most people, my moods go up and down and I have noticed over the years that there is a seasonal element to this. Springtime is best, when the days are lengthening, new life is pushing up everywhere and the long wait of winter is over. Summer is filled with long days and much activity surrounded by nature. But autumn, despite its mellow fruitfulness, is the opposite. Darkening evenings force me inside much earlier, I have to light the stove to keep the house warm and there seems to be more night than day. These seasonal cycles are a natural part of our being – our bodies and brains have evolved to deal with them. But somehow, modern life makes no allowance for the changing seasons. Those with regular jobs are expected to work at the same pace throughout the year. Apart from the standard few weeks' annual holiday there is no substantial period of rest for the mind or the muscles. Some people just find the condition called seasonal affective disorder (SAD) a bit uncomfortable. For others, it can be severe and have a significant impact on their day-to-day life.[26]

Winter solstice and the other festivals of the Celtic year were important to the ancient Irish people as a mid-winter break from the hard graft of living off the land. Such festivals also provided an opportunity to bring the community together in a celebration of the earth. Perhaps the best known of the megalithic monuments is Newgrange at the Bend of the Boyne in County Meath. This massive burial mound, eighty metres in diameter, was built so that the rising sun on the shortest days of the year entered the chamber at dawn. Was this a way that these civilised people used to celebrate the turning of the year, the rebirth of the sun and the coming spring? Perhaps the surrounding forests were the scene of a massive mid-winter party. Or did it have more spiritual connotations as a way in which the gods would shine a light on the graves of the ancestors on these special dark days? The winter solstice is still celebrated by a few people, often sitting in a circle outdoors with candles to symbolise the returning light.[27]

Today, most people have lost their connection with the natural world. They don't need to build a wooden shelter to live in, forage among the trees and fields for food or even use wild plants for medicinal purposes. Children generally don't climb trees, build treehouses or light fires because they are too distracted by modern technology. And we seem to have lost another benefit of woodlands which is the peace and tranquillity that they offer to the adult mind. Sunlight filtered through the green colours of the tree canopy produces a restful background for our eyes. The cool air inside the wood is a relief from the blazing sun of hot summer days. Foliage blocks out the noise of traffic, farm machinery and other sounds of daily life, replacing it with the rustling of leaves and dripping of rain to the forest floor.

Whenever I get fed up with work or world news or my brain gets addled by too many things happening at once, I walk down to the wood and just wrap myself in its embrace. I stand still for a few minutes and feel the peace of the wood, sense its long life and stability, the strength of the old trees and the rejuvenation of new plants growing in the sunlight. I feel a sense of peace and contentment with my surroundings and I remind myself to live in the present moment. This is better than any medication and it is free.

Ideas like this have been used throughout the world by alternative medical practitioners but they are relatively new in Ireland. *Woodlands for Health* is an Irish ecotherapy programme, prescribed by medical professionals, of forest-based activities for mental health patients. Research has shown that exposure to the natural environment reduces stress and anxiety. When people are in natural surroundings, physical activity releases endorphins that help fight depression.

In 2012 the first programme under this heading was initiated by Coillte (the state-owned company) in partnership with several other bodies. I took part in one of these walks in the woods around Glendalough where the participants chatted and learned to appreciate their surroundings, helping them to put their worries and anxieties in context. One person told me that he found the whole experience a relief from the noise and smells of the city where he lives. In 2014 the project was evaluated by the Wicklow Mental Health Services and University College Dublin, which found that participants improved their mood by three-quarters and their sleeping time by one-third. For some, their thoughts of suicide virtually disappeared. The researchers also found a significant reduction in guilt, hopelessness and thoughts of low self-esteem. The programme takes a 'recovery' approach, one of the fundamental principles in Ireland's mental health policy, *A Vision for Change*.

I go down to our wood every morning to check if anything has been happening the previous night. It is really just an excuse to feel the sense of peace and quiet wrapping around me as I pass through the closely spaced trees. It is a time to myself when I can live in the moment, aware of the sounds, smells and touch of the sleeping wood around me. I feel the rough bark on the big oak tree, smell the bracket fungus growing on the dead alder and listen to the creaking of branch on branch where the holly trees stand so close together it is not possible to pass between the trunks. When I share these experiences with others, I hope that I am helping them to relax and forget their troubles too.

## Barking mad

Since I was a schoolboy doing bark rubbings in art class, I have always been aware that each species of tree has a different type of bark. I never paid much attention to identifying them by this character, tending, like most people, to look first at the leaves. But in late winter and early spring, most of the deciduous trees have not yet released their leaves from the buds.

I have been studying an old book called *British Trees in Winter*[28] and I have decided to test my ability to identify each species by its bark. As well as illustrations of the bark types the book has a scientific key that offers a long list of choices to help with identification. Now comes the practical test, and, instead of using a blindfold, I have decided to walk through the wood on a dark moonless night. As I slip onto the familiar path an hour after sunset, I stretch my hands out either side and feel the bark of the trees as I pass. Despite seeing these trees in the light most days, I find it remarkably difficult to separate the species by their texture. I notice that moss tends to grow mainly on the south side of the trees where it gets most light and the soft surface feels different to the touch. It gives me a clue about which way to go, but it is going to take some practice to perfect this skill.[29]

One puzzling problem with identifying the trees by the feel of their bark is that, like our own skin, the tree changes with age. With similar functions to our own skin, the outer bark protects the tree from the elements, from scorching by the sun or drying by wind. It also helps to ward off fungi and the many insects and mammals that would otherwise take easy advantage of the sugar-rich sap or the wood that it surrounds.

Different species of trees have very characteristic textures to their bark that influence what other species live on them. The deep fissures and crevices on the bark of an old oak or alder are a haven for many species of insects and spiders. These invertebrates attract birds such as the treecreeper which is a specialist bark feeder, hopping up the trunk and probing the crevices with its specially adapted, thin, curved beak. I once found the nest of one of these birds secretly hidden behind a sliver of bark that had become detached from the tree.

As their name suggests, bark beetles are among the insects that also depend on this microhabitat. The larvae burrow beneath the bark of various trees, with each beetle species making distinctive galleries, or passages, in the wood. These beetles can break through the bark's defences, carrying in fungal spores that the bark would usually repel. Even after a tree has died, bark can be a haven for all sorts of wildlife. Bats, such as the brown long-eared bat, sometimes roost beneath loose bark, and a multitude of invertebrates also live out their lives in the decaying wood.

Plants that live on the bark of trees, without actually causing them any harm, are known as epiphytes. Mosses are a good example. The texture of bark influences the plants that live upon it. In an old oakwood, it is common to see many other plants such as polypody ferns growing in the deep crevices of the bark. The texture of bark, and therefore the lichen communities, can alter during the lifetime of a tree. Young hazel has fairly smooth bark, and so attracts lichens that prefer this texture. As the tree grows older, the bark gets rougher and becomes more suitable for other species, including the leafy lichen called lungwort which does not survive in areas with high air pollution levels. It is not only the texture that determines what can survive on tree bark. The chemistry of bark is also surprisingly influential. Aspen bark is not as acidic as that of some other trees such as pine and birch. This feature means that it can support species of plants and lichen that might not otherwise be present in a woodland.

Few people are aware that the bark of trees and shrubs also have medicinal properties. The beneficial uses include anti-bacterial, antispasmodic, anti-inflammatory, circulatory stimulant and laxative properties.[30] Wild cherry bark can be used in a syrup to treat irritating coughs. Willow is well known as a source of salicylic acid which can be used as a circulatory stimulant and to treat leg cramps. The bark of guelder rose has an antispasmodic property that helps with menstrual pains. By coppicing trees, the bark can be harvested on a regular cycle without damaging the growth of the tree itself and the young bark is richer in active ingredients than older wood which tends to be thicker and more furrowed.

### Planting time

We have decided to have a go at extending our woodland up the valley slope by planting a range of native trees into the pasture that was previously grazed by sheep and horses. This will have several benefits – providing a link to other woodland in the area, increasing the cover available to woodland wildlife and providing our household with fuelwood and possibly some quality hardwood timber in the future. I have to select a range of native species to suit the soil types and drainage which is quite variable just in the two fields. In the wetter lower parts near the existing woodland we will use alder and birch which can thrive in damp soils. The bulk of the plantation will be sessile oak mixed with birch and then, around the edges, I choose to plant a smaller number of trees such as wild cherry which has beautiful red foliage in the autumn, rowan for its wonderful crop of red berries and some hazel that will make a lower edge to the wood and benefit from the extra sunlight here. On the steeper slopes that have thin, gravelly soils, I have decided to plant Scots pine even though these are mainly from introduced stock.

Pollen excavated from bogs across Ireland has shown that Scots pine was one of the first forest tree species to colonise Ireland after the retreat of the glaciers around 10,500 years ago at the end of the last Ice Age. For most of the pollen records published to date, it can be seen that there was a major decline in pines around 4,450 years ago and in many places the pine forests were overrun by growing bogs as the climate became wetter. The great root masses and occasional trunks of so-called 'bog oak' that are often seen lying on the surface of worked peatlands usually turn out to be pine. This species has a distinctive red colour to the bark. It is believed that the species became effectively extinct in Ireland around 1,550 years ago and with it went such impressive species as the capercaillie, a large black grouse and a suite of invertebrates that are dependent on dead or decaying pine wood.[31] Pine was reintroduced here from Scottish plants in the eighteenth century. Since then it has been widely planted in large estates and elsewhere. The Forest Service estimates that it now makes up approximately 7,360 hectares (or just over one per cent of all forest cover). It is also spread from windborn seed and is naturalising in Ireland again.[32]

For centuries this was believed to be the situation until an Irish botanist, Jenni Roche, studied a previously unrecorded stand of pine at Rockforest in the Burren, County Clare. Taking cores in the nearby lake, she found that the continuous pollen record from the lake sediments suggested a relict population of pine had persisted there from at least 1,586 years ago to the present. This theory was supported by the finding in the core of a fossilised pine needle and wood fragment, aged at 1,110 years, which demonstrates that the species was locally present at this time. Roche and her colleagues have therefore rejected the hypothesis that Scots pine ever became extinct in Ireland. Their work has shown that native pine survived continuously in the Burren, at the western limit of its global range, which was previously thought to be the north-west of the Iberian Peninsula.[33]

To plant the trees, we have organised a *meitheal*, the traditional Irish word for a gathering of friends and neighbours to help with seasonal tasks on the farm that require many hands. The volunteers set off down the field with enthusiasm, spades in hands, and bags of young saplings with bare roots. People seem to get great pleasure and satisfaction from planting trees. One teenager told me that he wanted to come back in a few years and see how 'his trees' were growing. I wonder what Ned would have thought of this band of young people digging in the meadow where he mowed the hay a century ago. It is not hard to cut the damp earth and place the roots beneath the sod, firming it down with a boot. Over a hearty lunch around a fire in the old wood, there is much chat and socialising. Guitars are produced with music and laughter filling the quiet wood. As the winter sun sinks in the late afternoon, everyone goes home tired and happy.

## *Promoting native woodland*

Planting of our new woodland is supported by the government's Native Woodland Scheme. This promotes the establishment of new native woodlands on 'green field' sites. I prefer this to conventional forestry although its objectives are long term and not for profit. I am sure future generations will benefit more than me, although I have the pleasure of seeing a new woodland grow. Apart from producing timber, the resulting native woodlands have a wide range of other benefits and functions, reversing wider habitat fragmentation, protecting wildlife and rivers, enhancing water quality and the landscape. They offer opportunities to revive traditional woodland management techniques, encourage environmental education and capture carbon from the atmosphere.

The government grants for native woodland establishment have been available under the Forestry Programme from 2014 to 2020 with a target of planting 2,700 hectares of new woodland and restoring at least 1,950 hectares of existing woodland to give priority to nature conservation. Disappointingly, only a fraction of this budget had been allocated by the end of 2019. It seems that the grants for planting these types of trees are not sufficiently attractive to many landowners who would be required to take land out of farming use, halting their agricultural supports on the land with little prospect of a commercial return on the investment. The poor uptake of the conservation grants may be related to the current paucity of broadleaved woodland in general. There is a serious need for future governments to commit to sustainable hardwood production just as some woodland owners did in earlier centuries.[34]

Another new development in Ireland is close-to-nature forestry, also known as continuous cover forestry. This is a management approach where the forest canopy is maintained at one or more levels without clear-felling. The distinctive element here is the avoidance of clear-felling areas more than two tree heights wide without the retention of some mature trees.[35] Natural regeneration is encouraged but this can be supplemented by planting if required. This practice is in its infancy in Ireland where short-rotation, clear-fell methods are mainly used to produce fast-growing softwoods, mainly Sitka spruce and lodgepole pine. However, it has been the norm in many other European countries for several centuries. On a visit to the Black Forest in southern Germany, I was amazed by how enormous the trees are allowed to grow in plantations and the extent of forests right over the tops of hills.

Hans Carl von Carlowitz (1645–1714) was the first person to clearly outline the concept of sustainability in forestry. His treatise on silviculture is a compilation of the knowledge about forest management at a time when the practice of harvesting sufficient timber for the mining industry was done by selective thinning rather than clear-felling. Today, the charity Pro Silva Ireland aims to develop and promote continuous cover forestry which allows more natural ecosystem functioning through diversification of age and species structures and the simultaneous economic production of high-quality forest products.

I have noticed that, since we started to manage former sheep-grazed pasture as hay meadow, cut once a year at the end of the growing season, small oak seedlings have been appearing all over the fields. I believe that acorns from our local mature oaks have been dropped by birds flying over the land and have been growing here, grazed down by the sheep, until the right conditions allowed them to flourish.

Natural regeneration can be more effective than planting in spreading native trees. In planting schemes, the saplings are normally obtained from commercial tree nurseries. These bring the risk of introduction of pathogens like ash dieback and they are often poorly adapted to local environmental conditions such as soils and drainage. By contrast, natural regeneration of tree seedlings occurs easily when the pressures of intensive farm management such as grazing, mowing or cultivation are removed.[36]

Oak seedlings put most of their energy into root growth in the first stage of life. Under ideal conditions, some young oaks can develop a taproot that penetrates more than a metre into the soil during the first few growing seasons, but soil that is dry, waterlogged, compacted, shallow, or too rocky can restrict or obstruct root growth. The long root allows the seedling to survive repeated browsing by animals and still grow into a tree when the pressure is relaxed. Direct seeding of acorns, one of the earliest techniques used for forest regeneration, offers several benefits including costs that can be about a third of planting oak seedlings.[37] In our old woodland, natural regeneration is already occurring in most of the clearings with tiny seedlings of oak, alder, birch and hazel germinating once the sunlight reaches them.

### How important are native trees?

Naturalists are fiercely defensive of native plants and animals with an almost instinctive dislike of non-native or alien species. The basic argument is that wildlife which has been in this island since before humans arrived, about 9,000 years ago, are best adapted to the Irish environment and have evolved complex relationships with other species in the community. Introduced species, on the other hand, are those brought in intentionally or accidentally by people and these, it is argued, do not support the same diversity of native species.

There is a subset of the introduced category that are the most feared and despised types. These are the invasive species, plants like Japanese knotweed and animals like the zebra mussel. These can do untold damage to natural habitats and communities here as they often have no natural controls. Invasives like the American crayfish can outcompete the white-clawed crayfish and it has even introduced a disease to the native species for which it has no resistance.

The most natural areas are those that contain mainly native species and the loss of such areas underpins the current drive to restore our native woodlands. But which species are native and how is this defined? The first person to present the evidence for separating native from alien plants was Hewett Cottrell Watson in the nineteenth century. He divided the British flora into natives, 'denizens' (non-natives that grew in a completely wild state) or 'colonists' that usually grew close to human settlement or farmland.[38] This loose interpretation was updated in the 1980s by an Irish botanist, David Webb. He believed that far more aliens are represented as native and that there was a bias in favour of 'nativeness', especially for attractive flowers.[39]

So, what are the native tree species in Ireland? John Cross, woodland expert formerly with the NPWS, lists thirty-six species of native Irish trees and shrubs.[40] His list includes six species of willow, four species of whitebeam and a hybrid between the two oak species. There are two birches, silver and downy, and two cherries, bird and wild, on the native list. Scots pine has been promoted to native status on the basis that there are some sites with an unbroken pollen record since the last Ice Age. Some rare native species, that are little known by most people, include aspen, black poplar and the strawberry tree. The majority, of course, are broadleaved or deciduous while just three species, juniper, Scots pine and yew, are conifers. This group of trees is considered a high priority for conservation, not because they are rare in the world, but because they have been in Ireland since ancient times.

In eighth-century Ireland, the Brehon Laws divided twenty-eight native trees and shrubs into four classes of seven, based on their economic value. Described as the 'Lords of the Wood', the highest category included oak, hazel, holly, yew, ash, Scots pine and wild apple tree. For damaging one of these species, the most serious penalties were the forfeit of two milch cows or a three-year-old heifer, depending on the severity of the damage.[41] All of these trees had great importance to the early people – oak for its acorns, durable timber and its bark for tanning; hazel for its nuts and for the pliable rods used to make fences; holly as winter fodder for livestock; yew for making cooking pots; ash for furniture and spear shafts; pine for its resin that was used to make pitch for caulking boats and preserving wood; and wild apple for its bountiful fruit. Today, native trees are mainly valued by ordinary people for their beauty and their association with a much more diverse landscape.

But, as with the Irish national football team, there are many questions for ecologists about the native status of our trees and other plants. After the Ice Age receded,

Ireland was linked to Britain for a short time. So is a tree such as beech, which is considered native in the south of England but naturalised in Ireland, unacceptable as a native here because we are now a separate nation? Is this status just an accident of national boundaries? Equally, if the strawberry tree is found as a native only in Kerry, is the same species regarded as non-native if it occurs in County Antrim which is currently part of the United Kingdom? If a species makes its own way, by wind, water or animal dispersal to a new area, can this be considered a native in its new home? Should we not instead be considering geographic and ecological zones in the continent of Europe as the basis for native status? The question of the provenance of native species is also important as the seeds of trees from close to where they grow are more likely to succeed as mature specimens being genetically better suited to the local conditions such as soil, rainfall and wind exposure.

The difficult task of defining native status may be further complicated by the effects of global climate change which has already pushed some species further north and made the conditions here more suitable for trees that were formerly confined to warmer climates. Already a wide range of introduced deciduous and coniferous trees are used in Ireland for many purposes. For example, the wet climate of Ireland is well suited to several North American conifers which grow faster here than in their native continent. Sycamore is one of the few forest trees that can grow on offshore islands and coastal areas giving much-needed shelter to farmhouses where salt-filled oceanic winds would kill or stunt many of our native species. Non-native forest trees in Ireland can be controversial and often generate colourful debate, especially when the subject of fast-growing exotic conifer plantations is raised. Even more damaging are the pathogens carried on imported horticultural specimens which have caused epidemics such as ash dieback or Dutch elm disease in our native species.

More than 150 non-native trees, originating from outside the continent, can be found in European forests. The rapid pace of climate change makes it difficult for native species to adjust to new growing conditions such as increased temperature or more frequent droughts. In a few decades, some of the native trees, such as the oaks that we value so highly, may be struggling to survive in Ireland. So, should we be afraid of using non-native trees to restore our woodlands?

The most widespread non-natives in Europe are the black locust tree (*Robinia*) from North America and *Eucalyptus* from Australia, both of which are found in most countries and appear to have a wide climatic tolerance. This issue has been addressed in many other European countries and the consensus seems to be that non-natives have a place in reforesting the continent. One academic study looked at the experiences, risks and opportunities for non-native tree species in European forests. The authors acknowledge that these species may disturb ecosystems in various ways and spread unintentionally if the trees are not adequately selected or managed. However, naturalised species like sweet chestnut can replace native tree species that are threatened by climate change, insects and pathogens or other adverse conditions such as air or soil pollution.[42] Clearly, the climate emergency may require a radical rethink of our ideas on the primacy of native species in Irish woodlands and I intend to keep an open mind on this as we face into an uncertain future.

## *Spring – Rising sap*

The 1880s brought hope for local tenant farmers in this area. Charles Stewart Parnell, who was born into a powerful Anglo-Irish Protestant landowning family, lived in the local town of Rathdrum at the impressive Avondale House. As well as being a member of the British Parliament, he was a land reform agitator and founder of the Irish National Land League. He became leader of the Home Rule League, winning great influence by his skillful use of parliamentary procedure. The tenants believed him when he said that they would soon gain control of the land that they had worked for generations.

Ned Byrne's family was expanding and, in 1887 their fourth son, Dan, was born, joining the seven older children in the small farmhouse. The children helped by working on the farm, especially at busy times such as potato planting or saving the hay. Spring was also one of those times when neighbours would come together to help each other. Ned's brother-in-law, who lived in the neighbouring townland, would bring his horse and plough and together the two men could turn four acres in one day. The women and children joined in the effort, spreading farmyard manure and planting the seed along the trenches. Ned's family was fortunate that the river was close by, where his wife, Sarah, and their children went to collect fresh water every day carrying it back to the cottage on the pony and trap. Sarah milked the cows and made butter which she sold once a week in the local market.

The remains of Ned's rusting plough still lie today, half covered with grass, in a corner of the field. It has been a long winter, but the birds in Ned's woodland are beginning to tune up for the coming breeding season as I walk down the lane to the valley bottom. Woodpeckers are hammering on dead branches – a behaviour known as drumming – to announce their presence and territorial claims. There are jays about too, loudly arguing in the trees that have yet to produce any leaves. On one of my morning rambles, I find frogspawn in a still pond in the centre of the woodland. It has just appeared since yesterday, as if by magic. This deep body of water became part of the network of channels during the high river levels in the winter but now it is cut off again and becomes a quiet backwater.

The frogs must have been hiding in the vegetation for a while and I recall that I did hear a strange guttural sound coming from this direction several evenings back. Only the males croak. They call loudly to attract female frogs for breeding and to warn away other male frogs from their territory. Female frogs obviously think that croaking is sexy and are attracted to the pond. If there is competition between males, they will puff themselves up with air. Presumably, it makes them look larger and more impressive. If a female enters the pond all the males will try to mate with her in what is the closest thing in nature to our image of an orgy.

A day or two later winter returns briefly. A heavy overnight snowfall has clothed the fields and the hill beyond in white. The blackness of the woodland has suddenly become a maze of patterns as the trunks and branches are outlined with snow clinging to the windward side. As I approach the wood, hawthorn bushes along the lane are filled with redwings, fieldfares, song thrushes and blackbirds. Where have these noisy flocks come from? I have not seen them this year until now. My guess is that there has been a sudden influx from further east where the weather has been severe for days. Shortage of food there has forced them across the Irish Sea and I imagine the flocks passing over the Irish coast at night, taking them into a more benign climate. Birds use a variety of innate methods to navigate as, for most, this will be their first long journey. The pull of the earth's magnetic field, the position of the sun and the patterns of stars are all thought to be involved but this is poorly understood even by scientists. In the hedge here they will find what is left of the haws and perhaps they are also feeding on the clusters of ivy berries. The frost has hardened up but spring is not far away.

The first of the purple violets are already peeping out from the grass bank below the hedge. In the woodland there a few yellow flowers of primrose and lesser celandine to brighten up the gloom. It is the spring equinox, so I celebrate by cooking breakfast over an open fire in the woodland glade by the river. A steaming cup of tea keeps my hands warm as the dawn breaks above the eastern ridge. As I sit by the fire, a treecreeper is patiently working its way up a nearby alder tree probing in the bark for any insects that are hiding there from the frost. In severe winters these secretive birds suffer greatly as their insect prey becomes scarce and hard to reach.

The badger sett on the slope that leads down to the wood is surprisingly active in spring with much digging and clearing out of spoil and old bedding from all the entrances on the steep slope. The motion-activated camera I set up opposite the sett and it has recorded some short videos of badgers mating outside one of the main entrances. I call Enda Mullen of the Wildlife Service who has undertaken an extensive research project on badgers in Wicklow. She tells me that mating indicates that the cubs are being weaned underground and the female has come into oestrus and is receptive to the male – although it didn't look like she enjoyed the experience. There is no sign of cubs above ground yet but it is likely to happen soon as they grow hungry in the sett below. They will follow their parents into the nearby meadow which is full of earthworms. They must also learn quickly where the best feeding areas in the woodland are. Deadwood must be investigated for beetle grubs and the underground bulbs of bluebells and pignut provide a good source of protein.

## Carpets of colours

Spring is moving on and the carpet of bluebells that opens up beneath the hazel trees is one of my favourite pictures of the woodland in spring. As I drop to my knees to photograph them, the haze of blue is like a view of the ocean or the sky. Occasional waves of wood anemones or wood sorrel flowers form the white clouds. After the long months of dullness with monotone green and grey, the woodland is suddenly alight with colour and sound.

The bluebell is common in Irish woods although it does not prosper in dense shade or heavy growth of brambles. I think that the years in which sheep had access to our woodland kept the woodland floor open enough for them to survive. Elsewhere in Europe, bluebells are found only in Britain and parts of Belgium, France and Spain. Unfortunately, there is also a rival Spanish bluebell that is common in gardens and often escapes to compete and hybridise with our native species. Wild garlic or ramsons is the other woodland flower that I like to find, not just for its swathes of white blossom but for the delicious garlic smell from its leaves. It too has an alien competitor, the three-cornered garlic, that is very difficult to dislodge once it gets a foothold. I simply pull it up in bunches wherever I find it in our woodland.

The type of trees in the canopy influence the species of wildflowers found on the woodland floor. On poor soils under sessile oak, woodrush may be dominant while bilberry with its pale pink or green drooping flowers can also be abundant. Frauchans, the fruit of the bilberry, are a delicious addition to an autumn breakfast, but they are limited to acid woodland soils so I have to make a special expedition to the upland valleys each August to collect some. Under ash trees, bramble or bluebell may be common while in wet woods, dominated by willow and alder, I am more likely to find meadowsweet or the giant yellow flowers of marsh marigold. In midsummer when our woodland is quite shady, the tall white umbrella-shaped flowers of water dropwort fill the channels and wetter patches of soil.

Even within a single woodland the soil type has a big influence on what grows where as it is unlikely to be of the same quality and depth throughout the wood. The riverbank has typical alluvial soils that have been deposited here by countless floods. On the slopes below the groundwater springs where the water is base-rich, there are blue spikes of bugle and many mosses that indicate the lime content in the underlying soil.

Woodlands offer shelter to sensitive plants that would not survive in the open conditions of grassland or hillside. But the loss of sunlight in summer is the price that a woodland plant must pay for shelter. The wildflowers of the woodland are totally dependent on the amount of light coming through the canopy. This is why so many of them flower early in spring before the trees have had time to become fully dressed in leaves. This strategy has been adopted by wood anemone and lesser celandine which both flower in March or April when maximum sunlight shines on the woodland floor and before the shadows come with the tree leaves in May. But if a plant flowers when the weather is too cold for flying insects it must find other ways to fertilise its seed. The wood violet has a solution to this. Some of its buds do not become petals and never open. They fertilise themselves inside the buds and produce plenty of viable seed this way.

The caterpillars of several typical woodland butter-flies, such as the silver-washed fritillary, feed on the leaves of violet and other early flowering woodland plants. The large caterpillars have been hibernating over winter in the fissures of tree bark, emerging in March or April to feed on the fresh leaves until they are ready to change into a pupa. The adults will not appear till later in the summer when they like to fly in open clearings. Here too the woodland flowers are often at their best and, when a clearing is created, there are certain colonists that are quick to occupy it. Rosebay willowherbs or foxgloves can rapidly fill a whole clearing dominating the ground flora as they are both tall plants with large leaves.

### Let there be light

Unlike the conifer plantations of the surrounding hills, I often think of our woodland as a series of layers similar to a multi-storey car park. I would love to be able to climb to the canopy high above and watch the animal species, from caterpillars to woodpeckers, that find most of their food here. Below this, at the level of the human eye, is the shrub layer with low-growing woody plants like hawthorn and willow. Where a mature tree falls, a gap in the canopy appears and sunlight allows these plants to prosper and fill the space. At knee-level is the ground layer, often dominated by brambles and ferns with water dropwort and bugle in the wetter areas. This contains some tree seedlings, waiting for the time when they get enough space and sunlight to take the place of a mature tree. It is also the main nesting area for many of the commoner woodland birds such as robin, wren, blackbird and chaffinch. I have to get down low to find the ground layer which is full of mosses and liverworts but morphs into a sea of wood anemone, wood sorrel and bluebells in the spring. Here there are many ground-dwelling animals such as beetles, woodlice, centipedes and slugs. Just below the surface of the soil is a thriving, vibrant community of invertebrates and fungi, helping to break down the layers of leaf litter that have fallen to the ground over centuries and liberate the nutrients that they contain.

Where holly is dominant in the shrub layer the ground is often bare except for a covering of ivy which can tolerate the dark conditions. Where invasive species like rhododendron or laurel are present in a native woodland, the complex of layers is completely absent as the evergreen aliens shade out the ground and shrub layers preventing tree seedlings from germinating, supressing natural regeneration of the woodland. Likewise, browsing animals like deer and sheep, if present in unsustainable numbers, will graze out the undergrowth removing the essential lower layers and leaving only an aging population of mature trees. Even these can be damaged by animals that strip bark from certain trees.

I have visited many native woodlands where these problems persist, and the future of the habitat is in serious jeopardy. One such area in County Wicklow is Derrybawn Wood, close to the early Christian monastic remains at Glendalough. The wood is rarely visited by people, but there is a huge deer population here and they graze most young regenerating trees. There is also a dense canopy of old oak trees and if any young seedlings do survive the grazing, they will not get enough light to develop properly. Although part of the Wicklow Mountains National Park, this native oakwood has little undergrowth and is like an aging community without children or a long-term future.

How can we manage a wood so that it recovers the natural, layered structure that is so rich in species? The first requirement is for more sunlight to reach the woodland floor. Due to the abandonment of woodland management in many places we have become used to dark, dense stands of trees where the summer canopy blocks out most of the light. Surprising though it may seem, seventy per cent of woodland plants require reasonable levels of light to flower and photosynthesise.

This is why so many woodland flowers like primrose, lesser celandine and wild garlic flower early in the spring before the shade overhead is developed. The remaining thirty per cent can survive in lower light conditions and only a very few, such as dog's mercury, woodruff and some of the mosses, can tolerate the darkest shade. Among the native trees, young holly is quite shade tolerant while oak seedlings require good sunlight, such as that in a woodland glade, to grow well.

It is well known that coppicing, with its long cycle of cutting and regrowth, opens up a canopy and provides some of the best conditions for woodland biodiversity. This practice mimics the effects of a mature tree falling, creating a gap in the canopy and allowing a shrub layer of hazel, birch, alder or willow to develop, depending on woodland type. Some tree and shrub seeds will lie dormant in the woodland soil for years waiting for a disturbance to bring them back to the surface and sunlight to stimulate germination. In past centuries, it was common to run domestic pigs in woodlands where they would plough up the soil searching for acorns and roots. This had the effect of retarding the growth of brambles and bracken that shade the woodland floor thus allowing sunlight to reach the soil with its all-important seed bank. But the pigs had to be removed before the spring so that seeds would germinate and grow without disturbance. Today many native woodlands are overgrazed by deer at all times of year.

This underlines the urgent need for management of native woodlands to increase the light levels and re-establish dynamic cycles of disturbance thus maximising their value for biodiversity. As well as wildflowers, insects and birds will also benefit. Woodland butter-flies like silver-washed fritillary prosper in sheltered sunny glades and rides. Of course, not all woodlands should be managed in this way as some are already subject to too much disturbance from human activity affecting more sensitive animal species such as birds of prey. However, most of our woodlands are under-managed and could do with some greater intervention in a carefully controlled way.

Knowing this, I feel justified in removing or thinning some trees, especially shade-creating species such as holly and sycamore in our own wood. Reintroducing coppicing of hazel in limited areas is also producing some beautiful sunny glades filled with wildflowers and regenerating tree seedlings. Some of the wildflowers may not be able to re-establish in the short timescale of coppice rotation due to their slow rates of dispersal. Seeds of wood anemone, for example, are dispersed by ants and may be carried as little as twenty centimetres per year. If we can get their habitat conditions right, I may give them a helping hand by collecting seed or digging up a few bulbs of bluebells or pignut and planting these in sunny openings. Nature has taken a bad hammering from people over the centuries and we need to do everything possible to restore maximum biodiversity.

## Bringing back native woodlands

Today most native woodland is in private ownership but some is protected in nature reserves. Some of it lies within the state forest plantations. Short-rotation forestry and soft wood production is the main business of the state-owned forestry company Coillte Teoranta. But it is not so well known that one-fifth of the company's land – about the size of County Carlow – is dedicated to biodiversity. Some of these sites are classified as habitats of international or national significance.

In 2006, Coillte began a project, with joint funding from the European Union LIFE Nature programme, to restore some of the best examples of several native woodland habitat types found in Ireland. These are wonderful areas, still relatively intact despite the fact that their nature value had been overlooked for a long time. This project set out to restore over 550 hectares of these woodlands, each of which had been impacted in various ways by human activities in the past. Nine sites, all owned and managed by Coillte, were included in this project.

Among the aims of the Coillte LIFE project were to develop and promote woodland restoration techniques, to demonstrate the relevance and value of priority woodland habitats and raise public awareness of the need for their conservation. However, Sean Quealy, Coillte Project Manager, was quite clear that this was only the beginning. Accepting an award from the EU Commission, he said

> Four years of the project is only the blink of an eye in relation to the lifespan of a woodland but, even in that short time, the native woodland habitat and vegetation has been very quick to respond to the restoration measures which have started the process of natural regeneration.

I wondered what has happened to these sites since the four years of concentrated project work was carried out. So I met up with the principal ecologist with Coillte, Aileen O'Sullivan, who oversees all the ecological restoration work of the company. She traces her love of trees back to her childhood as her family home had a wonderful, large garden. 'At the backs of the gardens on our road ran an old tree-lined driveway which once led to a big house. It had become overgrown and we called it the "treesway". We used to spend hours up there playing and we all loved it. It was a space away from the hassle of the world.' She has worked with foresters for twenty years and has changed her views on nature conservation in that time. Aileen says:

I have come to recognise that all forests have value for nature, not only the native woodlands. My training in botany did not recognise that fact, but I now believe it to be true. I also have deepened my understanding of the practical realities of what it takes to manage a forest, and I believe that silviculture or forest management is vitally important. That knowledge and skillset is essential if we wish to safeguard forest habitats, and that is why we must positively engage with foresters in order to achieve nature conservation goals.

With Aileen, I was fortunate to visit one of the sites in the Coillte native woodland restoration project. Located along the southern shores of Lough Mask, on the Mayo/Galway border, Clonbur is the largest single project site, encompassing almost 300 hectares of diverse habitats. This includes well-developed limestone pavement covering the largest area of this habitat in Ireland outside of the Burren in County Clare. But a remarkable feature of this site is its range of other habitats. These include riverside woodland, heath, grassland, fen, lakes and ponds along with a well-developed woodland on limestone, much of which had been planted with beech and conifers. This landscape is unlike any other woodland I have seen as the soils are very thin and interspersed with bare rock which is incised by deep fissures.

Low levels of grazing have allowed the development of scrub-woodland cover over much of the pavement area. Despite this, some small patches of limestone grassland and heath persist, dominated by species such as blue moor-grass, ladies' bedstraw, wood sage, burnet rose and wild thyme. At the right time of year it is possible to find a diverse array of orchids, ferns and moss species. I had never seen such a rich limestone flora outside the Burren. Areas of dry heath occur sporadically throughout the woodland, with St Daboec's heath found, growing in association with common ling heather. This plant layer suggests a long continuity of woodland cover which is confirmed by the presence of broadleaved woodland on the 1830 Ordnance Survey map.

One special feature that I noticed at Clonbur is the occasional occurrence of patches of old woodland and some specimen trees, particularly oak and beech, a legacy of the former existence of the woods as part of the Guinness Estate. In general, planted exotic trees detract from the ecological integrity of the site, but the presence of well-developed stands of beech was viewed as a welcome additional feature to the diversity and interest of the site. These old trees support rare species, such as the bird's-nest orchid and the lungwort lichen. This mixed woodland community is also a habitat for the endangered lesser horseshoe bat, which is known to roost in the site. Therefore, carefully selected areas of beech trees are being retained here despite this being considered a non-native species. Throughout the project site, all other non-native tree species are being removed using a variety of woodland restoration techniques.

Aileen recognises that there is a need for longer-term actions by Coillte to maintain the restored woodland sites and to monitor the changes carefully to ensure that the work is producing the right results. Following the project, all of the sites were incorporated into Coillte's Biodiversity Areas and Nature Conservation Programme and these are monitored by ecologists on a six-year cycle. The follow-up work includes removing any remaining non-native trees or shrubs either as seedlings or regenerating stumps. Some seedlings of native trees such as yew need protection from grazing until they become well-established.

### Trees for bees

The sight and sound of insects in the trees is a welcome sign that summer is on the way. My favourite place to watch them is a sheltered, sunny corner where the path enters the wood. Here, there are several mature hawthorn trees that are covered with a burst of white flowers during late spring. It is a great place to find scarcer butterflies such as the comma and silver-washed fritillary. Bees, hoverflies and multitudes of flying beetles also gather on the blossoms to find the sugars that are essential for their survival. I love to stand for a while and listen to the buzzing sounds of tiny wings that are often invisible above my head.

All bees forage on a mixture of both flowering plants and tree species. Recent research has shown that honeybees have a preference for foraging on trees, even when these are sparse in the landscape. Trees and hedgerows are large and often unique features that help pollinating insects construct a 'cognitive map', making pollination and foraging more efficient. They collect this information on familiar landmarks during special observation flights and then return to share their knowledge with other members of the colony.[43] In the special case of honeybees, the hive is like an internet of precise information on good places to forage. Woody habitat features like trees and shrubs provide pollinators such as honeybees, bumblebees, solitary bees and hoverflies with a large proportion of their diet. Grassland flowers are also valuable but these are spread out in just two dimensions while flowering trees, with their height above ground and dense canopies in woodland, offer a much larger surface area for the same area of land. Part of the reason for the lack of understanding of this benefit is the difficulty of studying insects in the canopy of woodlands.

I climb into the branches of one of the old crack willows on the wetter edge of our woodland. The spring sunshine is beaming through the twigs before the first of the year's leaves emerge. The yellow pollen-covered catkins of the willow, that my mother used to call 'pussy willows', first appear in February in warm areas and continue until May in colder corners. The long flower clusters are filled with nectar that the insects carry to other trees for pollination. Within less than two months after pollination, willow seeds are ripe and ready to begin another reproductive cycle. Early flowering trees such as hazel and willow are especially valuable to pollinators when there are few other flowers in the landscape and resources are scarce after a long, hungry winter. The dangling golden catkins on the hazels and alders catch the spring sunlight.

These are followed by the white flowers of blackthorn and then hawthorn or 'maybush'. The white and pink flowers of bramble are widespread in the undergrowth making this a particularly valuable food plant for many insects including butterflies, moths and hoverflies as well as bees. Elder, rowan, wild rose, honeysuckle and gorse all take their turn in a cascade of colour and abundance for the insects. Even the green flowers of oak and the pink-tipped blossoms of ash have a role in the food provisioning. By late summer and autumn, insect populations are burgeoning and the beehives are full of larvae but flowers are scarce in the fields. Few trees flower at this time but a single strawberry tree (*Arbutus*) in our garden is covered in bell-shaped flowers, offering an isolated bonanza for the bees. This is a native tree but limited in its natural distribution in Ireland to the limestones of the west and south-west.

I am a great fan of the All-Ireland Pollinator Plan[44] which has stimulated people all over Ireland to encourage wildflowers as food for threatened bees and other insects, sometimes quite simply by reducing the frequency of mowing in summer. Pollinators provide what are increasingly called 'ecosystem services' but the role of trees and woodland in supporting these services has been widely overlooked.

## Climber controversy

As I walk through the mature trees, I often have to pull aside a curtain of climbing plants that use the tree trunks for support. Ivy is the main climbing plant that clothes many of the trees in the wood. It is one of the most misunderstood of Irish plants and I frequently have to explain to people that it does not 'strangle' trees or 'suck the life out of them'. The language that people use for these native climbers is reminiscent of the descriptions of plague or murdering invaders.

Ivy is a native Irish species that can tolerate dense shade and often covers the ground where other light-loving plants cannot survive. But, like all green plants, ivy needs sunlight for photosynthesis so it uses its flexible stem to climb the trees towards the sun. Twisting around, it climbs into the canopy and can form great clusters of evergreen leaves there that change the profile of the tree. But the roots of the ivy remain in the ground and the host tree is not harmed by its passenger. It merely provides the climbing frame. The cover of ivy stems and its dark leaves are used by many woodland birds for nesting in spring and by bats for roosting in the daytime. In autumn, when most other plants have fruit, ivy produces its yellow-green flowers, essential food for pollinators, and these are followed later in the winter by clusters of black berries, an important food resource for birds when foraging is difficult.

Like many other evergreens, ivy was believed in country folklore to symbolise eternity. It prompted people to believe in everlasting life and resurrection after death. Because it is not shaded by foliage on dead and decayed trees, it is often most abundant there and thus came to represent the soul which lives on even after the body has returned to the earth. It was also associated with cemeteries and gravestones where it was viewed as a symbol of mortality. Ivy growing abundantly on a young woman's grave was believed to be a sign of death from a broken heart.

Risteard Mulcahy, a retired heart surgeon, started a crusade against ivy in his book *For Love of Trees* which made a persuasive but flawed case against what he saw as ivy's disfigurement of roadside and specimen trees. He believed that ivy cripples and deforms trees leading to their 'premature death'. He made no reference to any objective scientific assessment and even admitted that 'the prejudice I have about the effects of excessive growth of ivy on trees and hedgerows is largely based on my own observations'.[45] Meanwhile, the acclaimed Cambridge botanist Oliver Rackham responded to this widespread belief. 'The notion that ivy kills the tree it grows on, can be traced all the way back to Theophrastus in the fourth century BC, without anyone stopping to think whether it can be true!'[46] In fact, there is no scientific evidence that ivy harms its host trees.

Also much-maligned is honeysuckle which is one of the first woodland plants to come into leaf in spring. The rich scents from its creamy yellow flowers in the summer are hard to resist. More attractive than ivy to the wildflower enthusiast, honeysuckle is also a tree climber. But, while ivy clings tightly onto the bark with aerial roots, honeysuckle grows more like a bean, twining itself through the branches to reach the light. The old name of woodbine describes the tangled, binding nature of the honeysuckle. It does most of its growing before the tree canopy blocks out the sunlight. Honeysuckle was once regarded as a symbol of fidelity and affection. A person who wore honeysuckle flowers, with their sweet scent, was believed to dream of their true love. It was also believed that if the blooms were brought into the house then a wedding would follow within a year. Perhaps it was seen to bind people together as well. The flowers are a source of nectar for many insects by day and especially for moths at night. The elephant hawkmoth is one of the exotic-looking species attracted by the strong scent from the flowers.

Honeysuckle brought out some colourful language from John Stewart Collis in his classic book *The Worm Forgives the Plough*. Born in Dublin, he worked on farms in England during the Second World War where he found himself clearing and thinning an ashwood in Dorset. He wrote:

> I have come upon portions of the wood where honeysuckle has practically taken over: the captive, the twisted, the mutilated, the dying, the dead ash trees stood hopelessly entangled in the network of ropes, pulleys, nooses, loops, ligatures, lassos which outwardly appeared as lifeless themselves as a piece of cord, but were centrally bursting with life and power, ready and willing to pull down the wood.

This, of course, is a huge exaggeration. Although the honeysuckle can mark the bark it does not cause the 'merciless throttling and strangulation' of trees that Collis claimed.[47] Some people think that wild climbing plants are untidy and this gives them bad press most of the time. But these are native species and all have an important role to play in the woodland community.

## *Watching the spring arrive*

Every morning I walk the same route through the woodland looking for signs that spring is really coming. Where is the first primrose to come into flower? When do the first buds burst on the alder trees and the delicate green leaves appear? Can I find the first frogspawn in that woodland pool under the old birches? When do I hear the first chiffchaff in song, newly arrived from its wintering grounds in Africa? Although each sign seems rather unimportant in its own right, I make a note of it in my woodland journal each day and compare with the same event in previous years. Is it earlier or later? Can it be explained by the hot weather of last summer or the frosts of winter?

The study of the timing of biological events in plants and animals, such as flowering, leafing, hibernation, reproduction and migration is called phenology. A Belgian botanist, Charles Morren, is credited with the first use of the term in 1849. Scientists who study phenology are interested in the timing of such biological events in relation to changes in season and climate. Climate change is happening all around us but the adjustments are often so small each year that they have to be measured over decades or centuries to show significant differences. Some scientists dismiss the value of phenology as not statistically valid or just a natural history hobby that has survived since the nineteenth century. They scoff at the lack of mathematical data and rigorous control plots, but the long timeframe over which some of this information has been collected makes it especially valuable to science.

At the Harvard Forest in Massachusetts, the timing of these minute signs has been continuously monitored at the famous university since 1988 by a forest ecologist called John O'Keefe. Like me, he has a circular route that he follows consistently through the year in the research woodland. He watches a sample of about fifty trees chosen to represent the range of species, heights in the canopy and different forest environments. He measures little but simply observes the timing of different events. Week by week he records how firm the buds of trees are, the first emergence of leaves, the first unfolding of woodland flowers. Leaf burst is now on average nearly five days earlier than it was when he started his observations. The onset of the first frost in the fall has changed even more, coming over a month later now and extending the growing season.[48] In Britain, the detailed records of natural events by the eighteenth-century naturalist Gilbert White have recently been compared with the results of two more recent phenology schemes. The spring flowering of many woodland plants, such as wood anemone, ivy, blackthorn and hawthorn, is much earlier now than in White's calendar.[49] These studies provide evidence of the effects of continuing increase in global temperatures.

Living on the extreme Atlantic fringe of Ireland, naturalist Michael Viney writes. He writes that trees may also take their cue for growth from lengthening days; their buds will open eventually even in a freezing spring. Similarly, their leaf-fall in autumn is triggered by shortening day-length rather than falling temperatures.[50]

I have noticed that some chiffchaffs and blackcaps are spending the winter in our wood where they used to appear only as spring migrants from further south. For some bird species or populations, the timing of events such as egg-laying and return from the wintering grounds is also changing in relation to shifts in the peak of food availability during the breeding season. A review of evidence from a broad range of temperate woodlands found that the dispersal rates of many woodland birds are themselves low, which could affect their ability to move to new habitat patches if currently occupied areas become unsuitable. Thus, woodland birds may be particularly susceptible to the impacts of climate change.[51]

The timing of emergence by insects is very closely tied to climatic changes in temperature and rainfall. It has been suggested, for example, that the earlier appearance of some caterpillars is now out of sync with the hatching of their main bird predators and this may lead to unforeseen consequences for both.

### Meeting the residents

I am discovering that the ecology of a wood is a many-faceted thing. The trees themselves provide the structure both horizontal and vertical. The soil is a key to understanding the type of vegetation and the way in which water flows through the habitat can be crucial to the survival of certain species. Listing the plants and animals in a woodland is just the first step but, like the process of valuing an art collection, it is important to get this inventory work started early. I can identify birds from their calls and this is often the only way to list the species breeding in the wood as they are invisible among the foliage. I know most of the native trees and a selection of wildflowers but, when it comes to the more difficult groups such as fungi or insects, I am all at sea.

Fortunately, a lifetime involved in natural science has left me with a huge network of friends and colleagues, many of whom are experts in the study of particular groups of flora and fauna. Among the first to visit the wood with me is Katharine Duff, a botanist and now senior ecologist in the Forest Service. As well as listing over seventy flowering plants she also makes a start on the ferns and mosses that grow in the damper parts of the wood. Exciting finds in that first season are the pignut and wood sanicle, two delicate plants that are indicators of old, undisturbed woodland. Together we see that the beautiful white flowers of wood anemones are widespread and abundant while wild garlic, which I have seen in many other woodlands, is scarce here.

Next to volunteer help is Angus Tyner, a local farmer and woodland owner who also happens to be an amateur entomologist. Together we lay out long electric cables from the farm to the woodland and plug in several moth traps as the evening light fades in the sky. These mercury vapour lights give out an intense beam that the moths find difficult to resist and they are drawn into a container where we find them in the early dawn. One by one, Angus releases the insects into the surrounding vegetation while calling out a string of beautiful and evocative names – burnished brass, double square spot, flame carpet, garden tiger, muslin footman, peach blossom, smoky wainscot – but the find of the day is the uninspiringly-named dingy shell, a rare species found mostly in alder woodland. At the end of a long process we have listed an amazing sixty-seven moth species in one night.

The fluttering moths around tree foliage provide an attractive meal for bats that emerge at dusk. I am joined on a warm evening by a former colleague Ciara Hamilton and her bat detector. Tuned into particular frequencies, the clicks and crackles of bat conversation can be clearly heard on this device. First to appear is a large Leisler's bat flying fast above the treetops. I think it emerged from the roofspace of a nearby house but it is hard to be sure without doing a stakeout. The Leisler's bat has a distinctive level flight from which it dives down after dung flies and beetles. This species is rare in Britain and the rest of Europe but it is relatively common here. As the sky darkens other bats begin to fly along the margins of the woodland gleaning insects from the foliage. They dip and swoop, circling around above our heads. Both common and soprano pipistrelles are here together, and they look and behave in similar

ways. They get their names because the latter echolo-
cates at a higher frequency compared with the former.
Both have a rapid, twisting flight as they pursue tiny
prey of midges, mosquitoes and small moths. A single
pipistrelle (weighing less than a euro coin) may consume
as many as 3,000 insects in one night. Pipistrelles are
frequently found roosting in houses, although they can
also roost in other locations such as tree holes. I am
aware that they will sometimes use old woodpecker nest
sites for roosting.

A wet woodland is an ideal habitat for bryophytes –
mosses and liverworts – that grow on the bark of trees,
on rocks and on the ground. Joanne Denyer and other
members of the Irish Branch of the British Bryological
Society have come in May to explore the wood for these
difficult-to-identify species. I walk around slowly with
these experts as they peer into dark corners, under
boulders and up and down the trunks of trees. Most of
the bryophytes need to be identified with a hand lens
but some are so tricky that they can only be separated
by examination under a microscope. The number of
species mounts during the day reaching a grand total of
sixty-one by the evening, including forty-four mosses
and seventeen liverworts. That's a good number for

what is a small area of wet woodland. Some of the species are relatively uncommon or under-recorded nationally. The key habitats for bryophytes are the springs in the upper wooded slopes, the wet woodland in the valley (on soil, bark, rotting logs or in streams) and on scattered mature trees at the edge of the woodland. Willows can be especially good surfaces for the growth of mosses and it may be that additional species will arrive as this is a mobile and changing element of the bryophyte flora. There are some old stone walls within the woodland that support a few additional bryophyte species. I guess that these walls were built more than a century ago by Ned, a previous owner of the land. All this effort to record the species that occupy our woodland is an attempt to understand the origin of the habitat and how long it may have occupied this valley.

## Origins of the wildwoods

It is difficult to imagine what this landscape looked like ten thousand years ago. But, with the help of some scraps of evidence I can piece the story together like a jigsaw. The last Ice Age had just retreated from the northern part of the globe and the climate was rapidly warming, just as it is today. However, it was starting from a much colder time when glaciers covered most of the country and little vegetation or animal life survived. During the Ice Age the land mass that is now Ireland had been linked to Britain and both islands were just extensions of the European continent. Large volumes of seawater were locked up in the glaciers and sea level was up to a hundred metres lower than it is today. But by now the ice was melting and vegetation slowly returned. At first it would have been tundra with low plants and lichens growing on a newly exposed ground surface that might have been frozen solid for part of the year. I was lucky to experience the arctic tundra first-hand when I joined an Irish expedition to east Greenland in the 1980s. The ground was still frozen in early summer and the air temperature made it feel like winter. Despite this, a colourful array of tundra plants stretched unbroken to the horizon.

In his classic book *The Irish Landscape* the eminent scientist Frank Mitchell described how the vegetation history can be unravelled.[52] When trees and other flowering plants produce their tiny pollen grains they can be carried considerable distances in the wind until they rain down onto the ground surface. Subsequent preservation in lake muds or peat bogs ensures that the history of the woodlands is recorded for later analysis. When a core is taken several metres through the mud or bog material, it removes a vertical record of the different pollen types being produced at any one time. The scientist (known as a palynologist) then produces a pollen diagram showing the dominant trees and other flowering plants.

Slowly, the climate warmed and temperatures began to rise consistently. Low-growing tundra gave way to heathland with crowberry. Woody vegetation began to return. First the juniper appeared – prostrate, gnarled and bearing berries in the autumn that could have been eaten by birds and small mammals. This began the expansion of woodland that continued without inter-ruption until the high forests were established. Mitchell believed that the soils resulting from glaciation were rich in nutrients and that luxuriant plant growth quickly led to the development of deciduous woodland. He pictured the climax of this phase as a time of tall deciduous woodland on deep forest soils.

But how and from where did the first forest trees appear? Professor Frazer Mitchell of Trinity College Dublin believes that the origin of Irish trees can be considered in three possible scenarios. Some trees may have survived the maximum glaciation. This seems extraordinary, as few other plants survived, but perhaps there were pockets of soil where tree seeds may have lain dormant over thousands of years of freezing temperatures. Others could have survived immediately adjacent to the ice during the main glaciation and thus did not have far to migrate back as temperatures recovered. Finally, they may have survived in refuges far from the ice edge and had to migrate back into Ireland with improving climate. Frazer Mitchell has collated pollen data from thirty-two radiocarbon-dated cores and used these to draw maps showing possible arrival dates, migration rates and direction of colonisation of the first trees.[53]

The early tree invaders seem to have migrated from the south and did not cross the Irish Sea. Hazel, which first appeared some 9,500 years ago, was one of the few exceptions. It was followed by Scots pine which first appeared along the south coast of Ireland around 9,500 years ago and had spread to the north by 8,500 years before the present. This is the timber that is most frequently recovered from bog cuttings today. Its identity is revealed by the red tinge to the bark when it emerges from preservation in the peat. Recent genetic evidence from Irish oaks also supports the likely southerly route into Ireland of this king of trees. Between 9,000 and 8,000 years before the present, oak had spread right across the island.

What did the primaeval forests in Ireland look like? Oliver Rackham, of Cambridge University, described two alternative theories for the appearance of the ancient wildwood.[54] The traditional theory, propounded by Sir Arthur Tansley in 1939, envisaged the country covered, from coast to coast and far into the mountains, with dense forest.[55] The second and contrasting theory is that the landscape was patchy and constantly changing with large areas of grassland kept open by herds of deer and other large grazing animals. This was put forward by Dutch ecologist Franz Vera in 2000.[56] Comparisons have been made between early Irish forests and those in the primaeval forest of Bialowieza in Poland today. Whichever picture we have in our minds, there were then a lot more trees in the landscape than survive today. The mature deciduous forests of oak and birch were undoubtedly rich in other species too. In the understorey, hazel, rowan and holly were important. The ground flora would have been rich in ferns, mosses and liverworts especially on the wetter western edges of the country.

There is also a suggestion that woodpeckers were in Ireland when the forests stretched across the country.

### Drummers in the wood

For several springs now I have been listening to woodpeckers in our own wood. They play their deadwood drums incessantly each morning as I approach the woodland but I still don't know if they breed here. Then, as I walk beneath the trees the drumming stops in one place and starts in another. Long periods of silence are their way of confusing me. They move through the tops of the trees with lightning speed but never give me a clear view. However, this year, I have started to find woodpecker nest holes. The first one is in a broken alder trunk about four metres from the ground. In fact, there are two holes in the one tree with one just above the other. I find a good vantage point where I can remain motionless and watch this tree carefully. For several days there has been nothing and then, with no warning, a starling emerges from one of the holes and is quickly replaced by the other member of the pair who takes up incubation duties. I have read that starlings can often take over old nest holes of the original sculptor because their season starts several weeks earlier. But the woodpeckers may return and attack the starlings, ejecting them from the nest site.[57] Not this year though, as the silence of incubation is replaced by an increasing clamour of starling chicks inside the tree. The feeding visits of the adult starlings become more frequent as they fly the same direct line from the woodland to some productive food source, perhaps at a local stable, several fields away.

Up to the present century woodpeckers were virtually unknown in Ireland and there was no conclusive evidence that they had ever bred here. Despite birdwatching for over fifty years I had never seen nor heard one until recently. Bones of the great spotted woodpecker had been found in caves over a century ago in two locations in County Clare suggesting that they were present in the Bronze Age. The finder, R.F. Scharff, wrote 'there are two small femora [femurs] somewhat peculiar in shape which agree so closely in form and size with that of the great spotted woodpecker that I feel justified in adding this to the list'.[58] But this could have been a vagrant bird blown off course and a couple of bones does not prove breeding here. Because they are so common and widespread in the neighbouring island of Britain it has always been assumed that they had died out with the wholesale clearance of our native woodlands over the millennia. Then, in a dramatic discovery, a juvenile bird was seen in a garden in County Down in 2006 but it took a further three years for the first occupied nests to be found in woodlands in County Wicklow.

I went to visit the site of one of the first recorded woodpecker nests at Tomnafinnoge Wood along the banks of the River Derry. From the size and age of the mature oaks I sensed immediately that this was a special place. This is one of the few surviving fragments of the great Coollattin Woods that once covered many square kilometres around the village of Shillelagh in the south of the county. In 1608 it was estimated that these extensive woods 'could furnish the crown with timber for shipping for the next twenty years'. In 1634 this area was described as having 'an abundance of woods, more than many thousand acres'. In 1670, it was reported that the Shillelagh woods were still extensive being 'nine or ten miles in length'.[59] But these fine woods were virtually extinguished by the early twentieth century, along with much of the native woodland in the country. Today, the last remnant of old woodland at Tomnafinnoge is relatively open with large gaps between the mature oak trees. Bilberry

grows abundantly between the trunks and in May
there are swathes of bluebells. Sure enough, I see the
tell-tale signs of feeding woodpeckers – a dead branch
that looks like it has been raked with automatic gunfire
– and I hear their drumming echo through the trees.
But the birds themselves elude me as usual. By 2015 a
total of 148 woodpecker nests were known in seven
counties in Ireland with over three-quarters of these
in County Wicklow oak woodlands.[60]

Back in our own woodland the drumming continues,
but my search for a nest has drawn a blank. Granted
I have found a few likely looking holes suggesting that
there were nests here in former years but none of them
seems to be occupied. Then, in the last week of May, I
hear a curious sound coming from a mature alder tree
overhanging the riverbank. It is a high-pitched *kee-kee-
kee-kee* but the continuous calling sounds muffled. So,
I circle the tree looking at it from various perspectives
wherever there is a gap in the foliage. About four metres
from the ground there is definitely a circular hole that
looks fairly well used so I make a crude hide from some
ivy branches and wait. My heart takes a leap as an
adult woodpecker starts calling loudly above my head.
I'm sure it has seen me but, nevertheless, it flies to the

hole and lands on a branch beside it. The response from inside is immediate and one well-grown chick pokes its head out of the hole to receive a large white grub proffered by its parent. Success! I have proof of breeding woodpeckers in our woodland.

The feeding visits by the parents are frequent now with a delivery every one to two minutes. Sometimes the meal is a large insect grub, occasionally spiced up with a beakful of winged insects. Once or twice an hour an adult enters the hole and emerges with a faecal sack – nature's version of the disposable nappy – which it drops as it flies off. For a few mornings I follow closely the fortunes of the woodpecker family but my excitement is short-lived. In the first days of June it rains persistently and when it stops one evening, I go down to the nest site but there are no woodpeckers around the tree and all is silent. I think they must have fledged in the last day or so. There are no signs or sounds of the birds in the wood suggesting that they have probably moved on. I have a sense of sadness, as if some welcome lodgers have moved out without saying goodbye. But I am also left with a deep sense of satis-faction that this is, after all, a suitable breeding place for this woodland specialist which may have been here when the same valley was filled with native woodland thousands of years ago.

## Mapping birds

'Spring is sprung, the grass is riz, I wonder where the birdies is'. This was one of the favourite poems of the comedian Spike Milligan and one that rolls off my tongue at this time of year. Standing quietly in the wood in April, it is hard to ignore the cacophony of birdsong especially in the early morning. Against a background of drumming woodpeckers, the trilling calls of wrens are the loudest songs coming from the undergrowth on all sides of the wood. More musical and varied is the song of the robin delivered from low branches and bushes often above my head. And the beautiful fluting song of blackbirds carries across the whole wood. These birds are resident species, staying with us all year, although they are fairly quiet during the rest of the year as there is little competition between individuals outside the breeding season. By April, the first of the summer visitors are here. Blackcaps move in to claim their territories with a loud, scolding song that goes on all day, every day. Chiffchaffs pipe out their repetitive, two-note song from the treetops while willow warblers deliver a beautiful descending series of notes from the willow trees on the edge of the wood.

Once the full complement of breeding birds is in place the noise is overwhelming and it can be difficult to separate out the individual calls of each species. But this is the only way to make a rough estimate of numbers and breeding territories. In general, only the males of each pair deliver the full song and its purpose is to declare their tenancy of a patch of woodland to competitors of their own species. Each bird knows that it needs to defend an area with enough food to provision a growing family or sometimes more than one family of chicks. 'Keep out' is the main message of the song and the distinctive tune of each wren is designed to be heard only by other wrens. This is the basis of a breeding bird survey. I have decided to try and estimate how many pairs of each species we have and to map their territories even though the boundaries are invisible and probably flexible for the birds themselves. With a large-scale map on my clipboard, I set out on the path through the wood at first light in the morning. Many stops are required to hear clearly which species are present. I will return at least once a week, walking exactly the same route each time, to compile a total of seven or eight maps, each with a series of codes for each species. Then, at the end of the breeding season, I can superimpose these and produce a single map showing the clusters of marks of each singing male that tend to stay within similar-sized territories.

I have been doing this type of breeding bird survey for many decades in many kinds of habitat, all over Ireland. Woodland is one of the most challenging environments to work in as the birds are largely invisible in the foliage and song is the main identification method. In contrast to walking round a field, getting to each part of the woodland plot can be a tricky job if the brambles and low branches are dense. One of the most interesting sites I surveyed is a wooded gorge in Wicklow called the Glen of the Downs. The trees are mainly old sessile oaks but the main road that bisects the glen is fringed with mature beech and sycamore trees. As I climbed the valley sides between the trees, I had to strain above the noise of traffic below to hear the calls of the birds. After ten separate early visits, undertaken in the few hours after dawn before the traffic reached its peak, I was able to map and list a total of twenty-one species here with an average density of thirteen pairs per hectare. The five most abundant species were wren, robin, blue tit, chaffinch and great tit, all birds that anyone can see in their own gardens. Interestingly, these are all year-round residents while the summer migrants were represented by only two species, chiffchaff and blackcap.[61]

Most of the early ornithological books describe birds on a species-by-species basis. The first author to describe woodland birds by habitat was the curiously named William Brunsdon Yapp. He was an English zoologist who worked as a lecturer at the University of Birmingham and received an OBE for his scientific work. As well as his teaching and writing, he served on the National Parks Commission and on the committee that helped establish long-distance walking paths in England. A keen field ornithologist, Yapp was best known for his book *Birds and Woods*[62] that distinguished between the bird communities of different types of woodland in England. In it he says, 'there would be no fun in science if all the answers were known but the materials for writing an ecological history of woodland birds are more than usually scanty'.

As our own woodland is dominated by alder, I turned first to the section of Yapp's book that describes the birds of alderwoods. Deep in the English Lake District in 1949, he carefully recorded the birds of a wet woodland including some species such as tree pipit and pied flycatcher that do not breed at all in Ireland. Other birds that he recorded in this woodland were similar to those in our own but curiously he found yellowhammer, normally a bird of hedgerows, and meadow pipit which I usually find on the ungrazed meadows here.

We know that Ireland has less than half the number of woodland bird species found in eastern Europe and only about 70 per cent of those found in Britain. Despite the fact that Ireland's bird community is short of many species found in other European countries, we do boast two notable subspecies both found in woodland – the Irish jay and a special Irish race of the coal tit. It is suggested that the specialisation in some of these birds in Ireland is precisely because they do not have the competition from European species such as marsh tit, willow tit and nuthatch that feed on the same range of foods in woodland elsewhere. The Irish coal tit has a stouter bill than its European relatives, which might help in opening tough seeds such as those of the yew.[63]

I remember standing under an old yew tree in a Wicklow graveyard as flocks of small birds – thrushes, blackbirds, chaffinches and tits – gorged on the feast of scarlet berries. The seeds are poisonous to humans and domestic animals but the birds excrete them with no apparent ill effects. Yews are often found beside churches and graves and may have had some symbolism that we have long since forgotten.

## Sacred trees

Standing beneath an old tree that has been growing for centuries in our wood, I get a strong sense of a link to something higher and more mysterious. Perhaps it is the height of the branches, connecting the sky to the earth, living in two worlds at the same time. As one of the oldest beings still living in this neighbourhood it might even remember Ned's family who lived and worked here over the centuries. Early Irish civilisations revered trees in the landscape in a way that is hard to understand today.

The Irish Annals clearly show that a belief in sacred trees was widespread in contemporary Gaelic society. Typically referred to as *bile* in the early texts, these 'sacred' trees were often associated with Irish royal inauguration sites. Their exact role in kingship ceremonies remains uncertain but it may have been something to do with the *slat na righe* (rod of kingship). This was the principal ritual prop and symbol of legitimate royal authority and it may have been cut from the

branches of the *bile* during inauguration ceremonies. In
the twelfth century, the king of Breifne was anointed
with a rod that had been cut from the sacred hazel tree
of Saint Máedóc.

The important role that these trees played in Irish
kingship ceremonies meant that they were often attacked by rival dynasties. Brian Bóru, King of Munster,
suffered this type of attack in 981AD when the forces
of Máel Sechnaill mac Domnaill, King of Meath, went
straight to Maigh Adhair in modern County Clare,
which was the inauguration site of Brian's clan the Dál
Cais. Here, they deliberately targeted the sacred *bile*,
cutting it down and digging up its roots. Destroying
this tree was highly symbolic and a direct challenge
to Brian's kingship. The forces of Brian Bóru, who is
better known for his role in the battle of Clontarf in
1014AD, had earlier attacked and destroyed a sacred
grove of trees belonging to the Vikings of Dublin. This
wood appears to have been associated with Thor, the
Viking god of thunder, and its destruction by Brian
Bóru was probably an act of both religious and political
symbolism.[64]

In the Christian period, certain trees also took on
a symbolic role in religious practice. Best known are

the 'rag trees', often found close to holy wells. As these were sites of pilgrimage, believers would hang rags on the tree while praying. The custom of rag trees is still strong among Ireland's Traveller community who maintain many ancient customs that have largely died out among the rest of the population. The rag might be from a piece of clothing owned by someone who was ill and, when hung from the tree, it was believed that the illness would disappear as the rag rotted. Sometimes the rag represented a wish or aspiration which the owner believed would come to pass by displaying it in a holy place. I have seen rag trees associated with the ruins of old churches in Wicklow including some in the monastic sites around Glendalough.

The Celtic festival of *Bealtaine* marks the start of summer in May when the hawthorn is in full flowering glory. The blossoms were traditionally gathered before dawn in country areas and placed in bundles on door posts to ward off evil. Hawthorn branches were also placed over the byre door or across the horns of the cows to prevent 'milk thieves'. Irish people of the past clearly lived much closer to nature than we do today with plants and animals featuring large in their practical and spiritual lives.

## Living in the wood

The ancient people of Ireland were surrounded by wild woodlands for much of their lives and they depended on them for many of their essential needs – food, fuel, building materials, weaponry and many more natural resources. Living in the woods was as natural then as living in cities is today. I want to know what it would be like to live in our woodland so I am setting up camp in a small clearing close to the river. The ground is dry but covered in discarded holly leaves so I start by sweeping these away with a broom that I made from birch twigs. A hearth was the centre of domestic life in ancient times so I collect some flat rocks from the stream bed and build a crude fireplace over which I place a grill from an old, long-discarded cooker. The fire is my first priority to cook dinner. There is plenty of decaying wood on the ground but I prefer to collect dead twigs that are still on the trees as these have dried much more efficiently. Slowly building up the size of the fuel there is a satisfying crackling from the fireplace. Waiting for hot embers to cook on, I use the time when the flames are strongest to tie up a small tarpaulin between two sturdy tree trunks. This will keep me dry if there is a shower in the night. The smoke swirls upwards through the foliage as there is little breeze.

An hour later, I am full after a hearty meal of grilled trout and fried potatoes, and the fading light makes me think of sleep. Blackbirds are clucking loudly as they settle to roost for the night in dense undergrowth. It is getting colder as I fold out my camp bed and slip into the sleeping bag fully clothed. The moon is out now, lighting up the woodland clearing with a yellow glow, as the fire smoulders and reduces to red embers. There is a cracking noise in the upper part of the wood. Perhaps the badgers are out now foraging for bluebell bulbs and may come past me for a drink in the river. The quiet rippling of the water over stones fills the silence as I finally drift off into light sleep. The pioneer naturalist John Muir wrote 'Come to the woods, for here is rest. There is no repose like that of the green deep woods.'[65]

My dreams are filled with fantasies of living permanently in the wood. Could I survive the winter without the comforts of a modern house? How would I keep the rain off and what would I do if the river were to burst its banks and wash away the campsite? The answer must include a tree house but where will I find the right tree? It needs to be a solid old tree with multiple trunks so that it will support the base of the house without pulling it apart in a storm. But the construction is for another day. Deep sleep comes at last as my mind relaxes in the peace of the wood.

*Summer – Forest flowering*

The early years of the twentieth century were a quiet time in this townland. The line of oak trees along the road were fully mature and in summer their ample spread cast a shadow on the people below. The trees would have witnessed old Ned Byrne, the tenant on this land, passing slowly by on his pony and trap. In his sixties now, Ned had handed over most of the farm work to his older sons while his youngest son, Dan, worked for the Glanmore Estate cutting oak and sweet chestnut coppice in the local forests. Although he rarely said the words, Ned loved this place where life seemed to be unchanged for as long as he could remember. But his own life was about to change forever.

He was going to the village, along with many of his

neighbours, to attend a meeting where he would have the opportunity to buy his holding from the landlord. For generations, his family had no more security here than a one-year lease on the few acres of pasture for their cows and a small field of potatoes. The land and the stone cottage, with its thatch of oat straw, were not owned by him but by the family in the big house down by the Glen. Like his father before him, Ned had spent his life improving the farm, saving hay in the meadow and selling a few animals each year to pay the rent. Apart from some provisions like flour and salt they were mostly self-sufficient. In a few years he would no longer be just a tenant as his father and grandfather had been but would have paid for the land in lieu of rent. Now, at last, Ned could become the owner of this small corner of the landscape that he called home and pass it on to future generations.

Dawn comes early now and I can have a good walk before breakfast while most of the local population is still asleep. I saw the vixen out foraging this morning and I guess she must have cubs in her earth in the wood. Already there are blackbird chicks in a nest as I have seen adults carrying food into a bramble thicket. The summer solstice in June is when the sun reaches its highest position in the sky and this is the day with the longest period of daylight. I wake up to bright sunlight and feel sleepy before it is fully dark.

My morning walk in the low sunshine is accompanied by a cacophony of birdsong from residents and migrants together. In the fields on all sides the bleating of lambs, already becoming independent of their mothers, is the dominant sound of the summer morning. Rabbits are out foraging along the sides of the laneway to the wood. Violets peep out from the shady places in the hedge and down along the woodland edge. In the warming sun, bumblebees flit among the golden flowers of gorse and white blossom of hawthorn. The meadow is growing tall and new flowers appear every day.

The wood is full of anemones and there are delicate green leaves everywhere. As I enter the woodland early in the morning a buzzard rises slowly out of the trees, calling and circling above the canopy. Last week it took off from the ground in a clearing and I found the plucked remains of a magpie where it had been feeding. This year I am beginning to think they may be breeding in the woodland, if not in our part, perhaps in the neighbour's section. I search carefully, stopping often to scan the treetops, many of which are still bare. Is that cluster of ivy twigs in a high fork dense enough to support a nest? A few decades ago, it would have been unusual to see a buzzard at all in Wicklow. But better control on the use of poisons, especially by sheep farmers, has led to a remarkable resurgence in the species right across Ireland. The familiar mewing calls of buzzards hang in our valley most days and the birds are breeding in many of the local woods.

## Midsummer deluge

The rain batters on the roof all evening searching for holes and pours over the sides of the gutters. It bounces from the road and washes weeks of accumulated debris along the drains. I can't see far as heavy clouds lie low over the hill and darkness comes earlier than usual for the time of year. All through the short night hours, the deluge continues and I wake early, excited to see how the land has changed while I slept. A few drips remain but the clouds have passed and the dawn light pokes through the morning mist. It is time to go outside and see what has happened.

I skip breakfast and release Molly my dog to run through the meadow. Boots are useless as the long grass soaks my trousers to the thighs. A mist hangs over the bottom of the field like steam rising from a river. Clouds of miniature moths flutter from the grass and swallows dip low to catch the swarms of hatching flies. A cock pheasant is startled from its grassy hiding place and flies noisily into the wood. As I enter the trees there are drips everywhere and the leaves take on a new freshness and shiny colour. The paths that were dry and solid yesterday have become muddy and soft. The river has risen during the night and where there was a bubbling channel yesterday is now a rushing muddy torrent. Side channels that are dry the rest of the year have become streams as last winter's fallen leaves are washed down into the river. Most of the plank bridges that I have laid across the channels have been lifted by the night's torrent and carried off downstream.

I stand beneath my favourite birch tree on the dryer slopes and listen to the sounds. Drips fall from the leaves. The birdsong is amplified by the mist and travels further than usual. A wren belts out an alarm call to its family of fledglings hiding in the undergrowth. In the distance, a willow warbler performs its cadence of descending notes. The weight of the downpour during the night has smashed tall hemlock stems which lie in the pools of muddy water. The woodland trees will drink up this unexpected summer refreshment through their roots and leaves and the young saplings will put on inches of growth. I leave the wood through the wet bracken disturbing clouds of butterflies and following the muddy footprints of a deer and her tiny fawn. She has made it across the field under cover of darkness and into the marsh beyond.

## Deer in the woodlands

There are fresh deer tracks in the mud of the woodland paths for days after the rain. As they are mainly active in darkness, I decide to take some infrared photographs to see how many deer we have. I set up my motion sensor camera one evening about a metre from the ground on a small tree. This relatively cheap technology is being widely used now by ecologists for monitoring mammals as they are mainly nocturnal in their activities. The siting is important, as the movement of grass or leaves in the breeze can sometimes set the camera running. Normally, I set it to take a one-minute video clip which shows not just the presence of the animals, but some interesting behaviour too. Next morning, I head down to the wood full of anticipation and, sure enough, the images loaded on my laptop clearly show an adult

female sika deer and her fawn browsing the vegetation
in a clearing. Examining the plants, I find that they
especially seem to like the new shoots of holly that are
emerging from stumps of the large trees cut last winter.
They also like to eat the fresh leaves of willow and some
of the hazel regrowth from the coppiced trees. I am
worried that this is going to get out of hand so I start
to put plastic deer guards over any young oak seedlings
that I find in the clearings. But it is impossible to protect
everything. I am finding regenerating seedlings of hazel,
holly, alder and birch in both of the clearings we made
during the winter. Sycamore and ash seedlings are so
common they litter the ground in some places.

For weeks I find deer tracks and collect photographs
in various parts of the wood and it always seems to be
the one sika adult and her young fawn. This species
is native to Japan but was first imported into Ireland
in the mid-nineteenth century by the owner of the
Powerscourt Estate in County Wicklow. At first they
were kept in a fenced deerpark but, inevitably, some
escaped and they interbred with the native red deer
that roamed the Wicklow hills and woods. Now there
are few controls and they have spread throughout the
lowlands too. When some of the buds are eaten off

the new hazel plants in our wood, I start to think of more drastic measures to get rid of the deer. I couldn't justify shooting a lactating mother and her young fawn, even if sika deer are considered an invasive species in Ireland. I could introduce some noisy device such as a gas banger but, like birds in cereal crops, the deer would probably come to ignore this when they realise that it is no real threat. I even consider requesting wolf dung from the zoo and placing this around the wood in the hope that the deer would have some genetic memory of this predator, which was last seen in Wicklow in the seventeenth century.

Then, as suddenly as they appeared, there are no more deer footprints. It looks like the young animal is now large enough and more agile for the mother to risk moving across open country and they have left our wood. The experience of the last month has shown me that if there were just a few more deer in the woodland over a longer period, the regeneration of the native trees I am trying to encourage would be put in jeopardy. I am also a bit worried because muntjac deer have recently been introduced to east Wicklow and the evidence from Britain is that, when they become established, they can do a lot of damage to woodland regeneration. By 2015 there were also records of these animals from various counties from Antrim to Cork.[66] Once established they are virtually impossible to control as there are no natural predators and the muntjac can hide in undergrowth where they are not easily seen by hunters.

In 2009 the organisation Woodlands of Ireland commissioned a comprehensive review of deer in woodlands as a basis for a proper strategy in dealing with the issue of deer damage to woodlands. The authors (forester Paddy Purser, ecologist Faith Wilson and zoologist Ruth Carden) concluded that the populations of the three most common species of deer in Ireland – red, fallow and sika – are increasing rapidly and in many areas are already at unsustainable levels.[67] Their report found that deer browsing is currently impacting significantly on both the economic and biodiversity values of forest habitats and predicted that these impacts will reach catastrophic levels in the next ten years if the current system of lack of management remains unchanged. These experts believe that the consequences of not addressing deer management will result in a whole catalogue of negative impacts: deteriorating conservation value of native woodland; reduction in hardwood and conifer wood quality; inability for broadleaf woodlands to regenerate thereby compromising their future viability; damage to agricultural crops as a result of increasing deer grazing pressure; severe difficulties regarding the control of disease outbreaks such as foot-and-mouth; and an increase in collisions between motor vehicles and deer, which may result in serious injuries or death for the motorists involved.

A decade later there is still no national deer management policy in Ireland and no coordinated system of deer population census or density measurement. Deer population management in Ireland is not practised to any significant extent and foresters and forest owners have an ill-founded reliance on recreational hunters to achieve the necessary levels of deer management. This will only be achieved through the use of professional deer management personnel. Without a proper domestic market for venison there is little chance of sustainable deer management, given the high cost of carcass disposal and the need for a disproportionate cull of females over males, for which some sporting revenue can be generated. The financial cost of deer damage is difficult to quantify. It includes loss of timber value, loss of biodiversity, reconstitution costs, potential EU fines for non-compliance with the Habitats Directive and potential loss of investment through failure to achieve the objectives of Forest Service grant schemes. Much could be learnt from our European neighbours where there are established deer management cultures, policies and practices. There is an immediate need for a fundamental change in deer management in Ireland. This can only be achieved through the establishment of a dedicated, statutory, all-Ireland deer management unit, similar to the Scottish Deer Commission or the UK Deer Initiative.

So, what exactly is meant by deer management? According to Woodlands of Ireland, it includes a number of measures, the most important of which is reducing the overall size of the national population by culling.[68] While popular images of deer such as 'Bambi' make this a controversial subject, it is an essential management operation in certain areas where deer populations are high. Wicklow is a good case in point where all three established species are present in high numbers and where the invasive species muntjac has recently been introduced. Culling needs to be done by experienced and licenced deer hunters who have the right equipment and safety training. The hunter is usually positioned in a strategic location, often in a 'hide' or on a 'high seat' with a good view over a clearing in the woods where deer have previously been observed foraging.

When new woodland is being planned deer fencing or tree guards are recommended to prevent deer browsing of the young trees in their most vulnerable stage. I have used both techniques with some success. The fencing is over two metres in height and special attention has to be given to maintenance over the succeeding years. I regularly check overhanging branches to make sure they have not fallen and damaged the fences. Gates are well secured so that they cannot be opened and the base of the fence is flush with the ground as deer are surprisingly adept at pushing under the bottom wire. So far there have been no breaches of security but I have seen adventurous deer crossing the meadow outside the fence in the early morning.

Deer feature frequently in mythology and folklore. Two tales of Artemis, the Greek goddess of wilderness, tell of her anger and the retribution that she exacted on those who trespassed on her territory. By controlling the weather, she kept King Agamemnon's fleet confined to port to avenge the killing of a stag that was sacred to her. A hunter, Acteon, used a stag's skin and antlers to sneak up on Artemis while she was bathing in the forest. As punishment for seeing her naked, she changed him permanently into a stag and sent him back into the forest to be hunted down and killed by his own hounds. In Irish mythology, Fionn Mac Cumhaill, the legendary leader of a heroic band of Irish warriors called the Fianna, cornered a beautiful white deer which his hounds then refused to kill. White or leucistic deer were considered to be taboo and not for hunting. Legends concerning woodland creatures featured prominently in past beliefs but these have largely been forgotten with the dwindling of the ancient forests.

### Where have all the woodlands gone?

We often hear that Ireland has the lowest proportion of forest cover of any country in the European Union. Why this should be, when Ireland has traditionally had one of the lowest human population densities in Europe, can be understood by considering the history of the landscape. The miracle of preservation of microscopic pollen spores from various tree species has allowed us to unravel the complex story of the ebb and flow of woodland in Ireland.

The first-known human settlement in Ireland was found at Mount Sandel near the mouth of the River

Bann. This has been dated at around 8,600 years before the present, at a time when the soils were becoming progressively more acid and less fertile, even then. This coincided with an increase in the pollen rain from alder, a common tree of wet habitats. It also marked the beginning of the Atlantic period that was probably wetter and warmer than the climate of today. Possibly, small-scale disturbances by early human settlers in the primaeval oak forests may also have prompted an expansion of alder at the expense of the original trees.

The first major forest clearances probably began in the late Mesolithic period, about 7,000 years ago, with the development of significant settlements. By the beginning of the Neolithic (or New Stone Age) the first farmers were already tilling the rich soils with crude stone implements and wooden ploughs pulled by oxen. These people belonged to a common west European farming civilisation growing cereals including early varieties of wheat and barley. They had domesticated cattle, sheep and goats and they used a distinctive type of pottery for cooking. Spiritual life was important to these people who spent considerable time and energy in constructing massive stone tombs from the local rocks and boulders.

The archaeological record is complemented by pollen records from nearby lake muds and peats which allows a reconstruction of the type of farming carried out and how this affected the woodlands. The oak woodlands would have provided plenty of foraging for domestic animals, particularly the early breeds of pig that foraged for acorns in the autumn and the underground storage organs of plants like bluebell and pignut in winter. As the undergrowth was grazed back, fewer young tree saplings survived and gaps opened in the canopy as older trees fell. The first evidence of cereal pollen appears about 6,000 years ago confirming that cultivation was underway.

A number of pollen records from Connemara have been used by Dr Michael O'Connell of NUI Galway, to reconstruct the landscape of the early Neolithic period.[69] As early farming spread, the amount of tree pollen fell substantially and was replaced in the record by pollen of grasses and ribwort plantain, a sure sign of cultivation and expansion of grassland. The woodland was replaced by pasture over large areas of Connemara with pollen of dandelion, buttercup and chickweed. This phase of intensive pasture farming lasted only about 150 years and was followed by a similar short period of woodland regeneration. Perhaps the human population declined and with it the level of farming activity.

In north Mayo, Neolithic peoples were also actively farming the land over 5,000 years ago. Here, in the Céide Fields, they laid out a huge area of small fields divided by stone walls in much the same way that farmland is delineated in western Ireland today. This activity has largely been determined by radiocarbon dating of ancient pine stumps preserved alongside the stone walls and beneath a layer of bog. The farmland was in use here for many centuries. A short distance to the west of Céide Fields is the Belderrig valley where the age of this farming period has been confirmed by the discovery of typical Neolithic artefacts and plough marks among the stone walls.[70]

By contrast with the poor soils of the west of Ireland, the Boyne Valley in County Meath is one of the most fertile areas of Ireland. The massive passage tombs, also dating from the Neolithic period, are the dominant archaeological features here. The Neolithic peoples who built these elaborate structures must also have had a high level of organisation. It has been suggested that there was an initial phase of settlement here beginning around 5,900 to 5,800 years ago, from dating of the rectangular houses at the north of the site. The main construction period of the passage tombs appears to have been between 5,300 to 4,900 years ago. In contrast to the agricultural landscape at the Céide Fields, which was fossilised beneath a spreading peat bog, the land at the Boyne Valley has continued to be farmed and modified by successive human populations, right up to the present. It has been suggested that the differences in the two contemporary landscapes are explained by the different types of Neolithic civilisation, with small-scale sedentary farmers living in the west and a more urbane society in the east with extensive travel and interaction with other regions of Europe.[71]

Some archaeologists believe that early people used the Boyne Valley for grazing of cattle in certain seasons and that there were large seasonal gatherings of a ceremonial nature. It may be that early farming was quite different to today with ownership of land being less important and people shifting around according to the availability of grazing and other food resources. This makes more sense if we envisage the landscape as largely forested. Openings were created in the trees by cutting and burning for grazing domestic animals and through cultivation of crops. With time, farming communities moved their activities, cutting down more forest to expose the rich woodland soils. Pollen studies support this model of Neolithic impacts on the forest with a dramatic fall in the pollen rain from elm trees around 6,000 to 5,800 years ago. This was followed by a phase of woodland clearance, then an arable and pastoral stage with later woodland regeneration and then further clearance activity.

So, when did the clearance of the native woods in Ireland actually begin? As soon as the Mesolithic hunters penetrated the forests in the interior of the country, they would have made small clearings on the shores of lakes and rivers as they cut the mature trees for firewood.[72] Perhaps they would have had temporary camps – in the hills in summer and on the lowlands in winter – to exploit the plentiful game. The impact of Neolithic peoples on the primaeval woodlands from about 5,000 years ago is certain. If the forests had been dense then they would have had to create clearings for their domestic animals and crops. If it was a patchwork already, due to grazing wild animals, then the early farmers probably concentrated on the grasslands first and gradually expanded these. Oliver Rackham believed that in Ireland (and Scotland) much of the wildwood was converted directly to moorland in the uplands and the west and that natural processes of climate change played a much greater role in the loss of the wildwoods here than in England. In the western areas of highest rainfall, woodland was replaced by progressive accumulation of blanket peat.

By 4,500 years ago the first Neolithic farmers made larger clearances in the woods for grazing and cultivation. They may have concentrated on the hillsides where the woodlands were thinner and the soils more free-draining. Upland areas may have been used for rough grazing and large burial cairns were built on the summits.[73]

By the end of the Bronze Age, about 2,500 years ago, the hills had been completely cleared of woodland by a combination of burning and cultivation. On the summits, blanket bogs had replaced the woodlands. In the lowlands, clearance for cattle grazing continued but the climate deteriorated and cultivation was replaced by forest regrowth. In the early Christian period, around 800AD, the population expanded again, new settlements were created in ringforts and the expansion of farming led to significant habitat change. Open fields replaced woodland and scrub and grazing in woodland clearings became extensive.

Of course, there is no accurate record of prehistoric people in Ireland and the earliest annals are filled with myth and legend more than fact. We must wait until the medieval period for the first real written natural history of Ireland. Giraldus Cambrensis was the pen name of a Welshman, Gerald de Barri, who was born at the castle of Manorbier in Pembrokeshire, West Wales about 1146AD. His mother was Angharad, who was a celebrated mistress of King Henry I. Cambrensis came to Ireland for the first time in 1183 with his uncle and his brother and 'diligently explored the site and nature of the island and primitive origin of its race'. It is known that he travelled from Waterford to Dublin. We know also that he passed through Meath and Kildare and he may have seen the Shannon including Lough Ree and Lough Derg. Little more is known of the locations that he visited.[74]

Giraldus Cambrensis kept detailed diaries of his tours and when he returned to Wales he wrote, in Latin, his great book *Topograpia Hiberiniae* (*The History and Topography of Ireland*). He described Ireland as 'a country of uneven surface and rather mountainous. Still there are, here and there, some fine plains, but in comparison with the woods they are indeed small.'

Cambrensis also reported the presence in Ireland of some typical woodland mammal species.

> We have never seen anywhere such a supply of boars and wild pigs ... There are many hares but rather small ... Martens are very common in the woods. They are hunted all day and all night, by means of fire. The badger or melot is also found here ... scraping and digging with its feet it makes for itself holes under the ground as places of refuge and defence.

He also noted the absence in Ireland of woodland species that were present in Britain: 'The island suffers the absence of certain wild beasts. Wild-goats, deer generally, hedgehogs and polecats are wanting'. He reported that 'there are only two kinds of harmful beasts in Ireland, namely, wolves and foxes'. Hunting and woodland clearance had obviously been going on since the first humans arrived in Ireland but it was accelerating now as the population grew.

Loading an oak log in east Wicklow in the early twentieth century. The tree from which it was cut may have been several hundred years old. (*Photo courtesy of Michael Carey*)

The road from the village to the woodland is lined by 200-year-old oak trees. They were planted by the landlord in prominent positions on his estate.

Snow on the windward side of alder trees highlights their intricate twig structure.

Woodsman Mike Carswell coppicing hazel trees in winter. This ancient practice allows the trees to regrow indefinitely, giving a steady supply of timber products.

Old oak tree in winter. Crevices in the bark are used for overwintering by insects.

Karen and Holly Norman among volunteers planting trees in former pasture. People enjoy helping to establish new woods as a positive contribution to the environment.

Oak trees in deer guards. These are necessary to protect the young saplings from browsing-by deer, but they will be removed as the trees mature.

A fern unrolls its frond in spring. Ferns are primitive plants that reproduce by releasing tiny spores into the wind.

Male catkins carrying pollen emerge on the hazel trees in early spring. The tiny red female flowers are also visible.

Wild garlic flowers early in spring before the tree canopy blocks
out sunlight. Its aromatic leaves make a delicious pesto.

Bluebells flower in the hazel woodland in May. They benefit
from plenty of sunlight in woodland clearings.

Wood sorrel is one of the
early flowering woodland
plants. Its leaves contain
oxalic acid, giving them
a sour lemony flavour.

Bog woodland with
birch trees growing from
mossy cushions. This is
a rare habitat, but it is
gradually regenerating on
cutover bogs.

A great spotted woodpecker feeds its chick in an alder tree.
The natural recolonisation by this native bird has been mainly
in native woodland in County Wicklow.
(*Photo by Declan Murphy*)

The author leads a
walk through the
woodland. Education is
important to help people
understand the benefits
of woodlands and how
they are managed.

A fallow deer listens alertly for danger. Deer can prevent woodland regeneration by browsing young trees and undergrowth. (*Photo by Will O'Connor*)

A mountain stream flows through a Wicklow oakwood. The woodland helps keep the water clean by intercepting nutrients from surrounding land.

Red kite with two well-grown chicks on a nest in Wicklow.
The survival of native woodlands here has helped the
reintroduction of this native bird of prey after two centuries.
(*Photo by Marc Ruddock*)

Silver-washed fritillary on a bramble flower. This is one of the
largest Irish butterflies whose caterpillar feeds on violets.

Hurdle fence and gate created by Mike Carswell using
native wood products including hazel and oak.
(*Photo by Mike Carswell*).

Fly agaric is one of the poisonous woodland fungi to be avoided.
Many others are edible, but accurate identification is essential.

The woodstore stacked high with firewood for the winter. This is a by-product of woodland management.

Holly and hawthorn berries provide a winter feast for birds.

Pine martens have returned to Wicklow woods after an absence of centuries. About the size of domestic cats, they eat a wide range of foods from berries to small rodents. (*Photo by Ruth Hanniffy*)

Red squirrels have benefitted from the return of the pine marten, which preys on their competitor the grey squirrel. (*Photo by John Fox*)

Alder cones contain tiny black seeds that can be grown in a nursery and the saplings planted out to extend woodland cover in wet soils.

The canopy of the woodland has an intimate mixture of native trees including alder, birch, oak and ash.

A badger emerges from its sett in the wood just after dark. Their
traditional breeding places may be used for many generations.
(*Photo by Karl Partridge*).

The author beside a large birch tree in the wood. Holly
undergrowth has been thinned out to encourage natural
regeneration of trees.

## River woods

It is high summer now and I welcome two woodland experts to wander with me among our trees. John Cross, formerly woodland specialist with the NPWS, and his successor, Jenni Roche, have both agreed to give me their opinion on how to categorise our small patch of trees. As it is regularly flooded in winter, I have long wondered if it fits within the definition of alluvial forest – a habitat that is considered by the European Commission to be a priority for conservation across the continent.

There are few large examples of this habitat type in Ireland but the best known is the Gearagh in County Cork. This unusual area formed where the River Lee breaks into a complex network of channels weaving through a maze of wooded islands. The area was probably wooded throughout the post-glacial era and frequent flooding has served to enhance its character. I went there once with the nature photographer, Richard Mills, who lives locally. Originally, this area of alluvial woodland extended as far as the Lee Bridge. Unfortunately, in the mid-1950s, in the eastern part of the Gearagh, extensive tree-felling and flooding were carried out to create a reservoir and supply the head of water needed for a hydroelectric scheme. Almost

two-thirds of the former woodland were lost. The
islands in the remaining part of the Gearagh consist of
alluvial soils and support an almost closed canopy of
pedunculate oak, ash and birch. We walked through
hazel, holly and hawthorn. Willows and alder are largely
confined to channel margins and waterlogged areas. The
ground beneath our feet was soft and muddy. The plants
of the woodland floor are rather similar to those in
our own small patch in Wicklow with an abundance of
wood anemone flowering in the spring. Scarce species
of particular interest within the Gearagh woodland are
wood club-rush, bird cherry and buckthorn. Moss and
lichen communities grow abundantly on tree trunks.
Variations in this vegetation occur locally, where drainage
is impeded and where tree clearance has occurred. The
whole area has a remarkably wild character, with many
fallen trees blocking the channels, so that access both
by foot and boat is difficult. Within the reservoir, the
former vast extent of the woodland is obvious at times
of low water; the cut stumps of larger trees can be seen
– like a graveyard of the woodland ancestors.

Back in our own woodland, there are numerous
channels that weave among the alder trees although
some of them are dry in summer. In places trees have

fallen across the channels, temporarily blocking the water until the river finds a way around them. I suspect that the main river may have been diverted in the past into a completely different path either by a large fallen tree or by human intervention. Jane Clarke, who lives in County Wicklow, has captured the beauty of these places in her poem 'When the tree falls':

> into the river
>> it slows the current
>
>>> water pools
>> in the hollows it makes
>
> pike and trout
>> find a new place to hide
>
>>> beetles mayfly and mites
>> feed on leaf litter
>
> the mossy trunk
>> lies still as a bridge
>
>>> a kingfisher settles
>> watches for minnow
>
> branches reach for the light
>> noble with new buds

The presence of dead and decaying wood in the
water itself also slows the flow, preventing flooding
downstream. Wood in rivers also provides a refuge
for fish and invertebrates, including the aptly named
Logjammer hoverfly. Riparian (or riverside) woodland
has huge benefits for biodiversity both in the water and
on the land. The roots of the trees intercept nutrients
draining off agricultural land in the catchment, trapping
these in the woodland soil. Up to 90 per cent reduc-
tions in nitrate concentrations in shallow groundwater
discharging from farmland have been measured in the
USA.[75] In Austria, riparian forest buffers have been
found to significantly retain excess nutrients and thereby
improve water quality in nutrient-enriched agricultural
streams.[76] Riparian woods can also ameliorate the
effects of many pesticides and provide dissolved and
particulate organic food maintaining high biological
productivity and diversity in rivers and streams that pass
through them.

I persuaded Mary Kelly-Quinn, a freshwater
biologist who lives in Wicklow, to sample the river water
in our woodland. Among the commoner creatures, she
found two species of mayflies and two stoneflies, all
indicators of the cleanest water conditions. I knew that

there were trout in the river but imagine my surprise when a sensor camera that I was using to film badgers showed the distinctive outline of an otter emerging from the water. These secretive mammals are much more likely to move along the watercourse under cover of dense vegetation in search of aquatic prey.

John and Jenni have lots to say about our woodland and I wait with bated breath for their pronouncements, like waiting to hear the result of a car test. As both are experienced botanists, they spent some time looking at the plants and reading through my list of almost eighty flowering plants and over sixty mosses and liverworts. They conclude that our woodland is in the alder-meadowsweet category, in a sub-division called alder-creeping buttercup, but with elements of ash-marsh bedstraw. I know from experience over several winters that the woodland is alluvial as the lower parts are subject to flooding and the slopes are spring-fed. This means that it fits within the Habitats Directive category of 'alluvial forests with alder and ash' which is a conservation priority in EU member states. This makes me feel even more protective of the wood as sites of international value for biodiversity are generally rare and threatened.

## *Scrub to woodland*

To extend our mature woodland up the valley we have surrounded six acres of sheep pasture with high fencing to exclude deer and livestock. Into this area we planted nearly 7,000 broadleaved trees. As these small trees have grown, I am amazed by the rapid spread of other species from the hedgerows since grazing ceased. New thorny whips of blackthorn and flexible stems of willow are leap-frogging the new fence and appearing around the edge of the fields. Brambles poke through the wire mesh, reaching out their growing tips to touch the ground inside. Even oak seedlings have started to appear where acorns fell in the autumn months. I am watching natural succession in action here, the process by which the structure of a biological community or habitat changes naturally over time. Grassland is only a temporary stage in the colonisation of bare ground by vegetation. Once grazing animals are excluded, grassland is often replaced by scrub.

These pioneer scrub species frequently produce large numbers of seeds which can be dispersed by birds or by wind. On a breezy day in spring the feathery seeds of willow drift like snow across our fields. In autumn birds feed voraciously on blackberries in the surrounding hedges and their droppings are packed with the seeds of bramble. Seeds generally germinate better in open grassland than in dense shade. Some scrub species (like blackthorn and gorse) have spines on their stems which are effective in deterring browsing animals like deer, sheep and rabbits, while others, such as bramble and dog rose, have long flexible stems that help them scramble over other plants. Scrub plants may also use asexual methods of reproduction; brambles, for example, produce arching stems and when the tip touches the ground, roots may be produced and eventually a new plant will develop.

The role of scrub in woodland evolution has become a major discussion point in the debate about how Europe's primaeval woodland developed. The classical view, largely based on the counting of pollen grains preserved in sediments, is that closed-canopy forest was the predominant habitat type before people arrived to create clearings. However, the Dutch ecologist Frans Vera argues that some of our most common forest trees, such as oak, are light-demanding and do not prosper under a dark canopy of the same or other species. Instead, he visualises open wood pasture with occasional large spreading oaks surrounded by grassland with roving herbivores and 'mantle and fringe vegetation' dominated by light-demanding shrub species. Acorns dropped by birds into patches of thorny scrub would have been protected from grazing animals allowing the oak saplings to develop in relatively bright conditions.[77] Whichever theory best represents the prehistoric wildwood, there is no doubt that scrub can help trees to survive today in intensively grazed land.

Hazel-dominated scrub is widespread in the Burren, County Clare. Thorny scrub species such as black-thorn, hawthorn and holly are often present and even make it difficult for the herds of feral goats to pass through. Hazel scrub was one of the key habitats where pine martens survived during the early twentieth century when poison and persecution reduced numbers dramatically in other woodlands. In some areas of the Burren the scrub has now developed into ash-hazel woodland. In other areas it forms a mosaic with patches occurring in open grassland. While mature hazel scrub is an important habitat for lichens and certain fungi, including the rare hazel gloves fungus, its rapid encroachment onto calcareous grasslands and limestone heath is seen as a threat to some areas of species-rich vegetation. In the mid-nineteenth century, when the human population was at an all-time high, scrub was extensively cut back to expose land for grazing. As agricultural pressure reduced in the following century, the scrub spread over land formerly grazed.

Within the area we had selected for our native woodland plantation we left a sizeable area covered with mature hawthorn and gorse scrub with ash trees emerging within it. We also left an area of developing willow scrub in a very waterlogged corner where dragonflies flit between the trees in early summer. These are also ideal habitats for some birds, such as linnet, stonechat and willow warbler. Scrub is a key stage in the natural regeneration of woodland but it is often overlooked or worse, removed before the trees can develop. Even the name scrub conjures up a picture of an untidy area of land and agricultural grant schemes often require scrub to be removed before payments are made. A better term for scrub is emerging woodland and this is the basis of a new element of the Native Woodland Scheme which provides grant aid to landowners wishing to encourage natural regeneration of woods. We are beginning to understand the potential of scrub to form a key stage in the recovery of the more diverse woodland types.

## Predators and prey

The relationship between predators and their prey is often misunderstood by non-scientists. I have frequently heard it said that small birds have declined because of high numbers of magpies or that the booming fox population is reducing the numbers of rabbits in the countryside. In reality, the opposite is true, as biologists have plenty of examples of predator populations that have declined because a key prey species is less available. When the disease myxomatosis hit the rabbit population in the 1950s, there was a significant impact on foxes which then turned to other available prey such as birds and even domestic poultry to fill the hungry gap. In dry summers, when earthworms burrow deeper in the soil, badgers have smaller families because there is not enough of this key prey species to keep them going.

When we felled a number of mature sycamores in our woodland many of the upper branches and twigs had bark damage which was characteristic of grey squirrel feeding. They tend to tear off the bark in strips between July and September to get at the sugars contained in the sap. This can cause dieback in these branches. So, I set up a camera in one of the clearings on a June evening to see if I could confirm the culprits.

To attract the mammals into range of the camera I spread some peanuts on a sycamore stump. Imagine my surprise when the pictures revealed a pine marten happily eating the bait in bright sunshine. Martens move just like domestic cats and they are very efficient tree climbers. They have a distinctive chocolate brown fur, a bushy tail, a white flash on the chest and creamy yellow borders to the ears. The only likely confusion is with the invasive American mink which is generally larger, darker and tends to live close to water. I know that pine martens are in this area as I have seen them on local roads but this is the first time I have recorded them in our woodland and I am pleased for a number of reasons.

The pine marten was a very rare animal in Ireland in the 1970s when I first started working in nature conservation. Once common throughout the country, by the twentieth century the species had become extinct in most of Ireland, surviving only in a few isolated populations in the west. The main reasons for the species' decline were related to hunting for its fur; loss of habitat through the destruction of forests; direct and indirect poisoning and persecution as a potential predator of livestock and game populations. But it has recently undergone a natural range expansion after centuries of decline. It is thought that plantation forests give it both cover and stepping stones in the landscape.

In 2016 a national survey was undertaken for the NPWS where pine marten density and abundance were assessed in nineteen forested study sites throughout Ireland, using non-invasive research techniques.[78] The researchers were able to identify individual martens from the DNA in hair samples that they collected and analysed. In most study sites, the number of individual pine martens detected was less than ten individuals. From existing information on the current distribution and area of forest habitat occupied by the species, the total population of pine martens in Ireland was estimated at over 3,000 individuals. This confirms that the pine marten is still amongst the rarest of all wild mammals in Ireland but it is making a welcome comeback. It requires careful conservation management to sustain the population and bring it back to its natural levels.

Native to the broadleaf forests of the eastern United States, the grey squirrel was first introduced at Castleforbes, County Longford in 1911 from English stock. Since its introduction it has proved to be a considerable pest in woodlands and a competitor with the native red squirrel. It is believed that the red squirrel has suffered a one-fifth decline in range since the introduction of its American cousin to Ireland, due to competition for resources. It seems that the larger grey squirrel is able to breed faster and competes with the smaller species for limited food supplies. I have seen grey squirrels in our own wood several times and the damage to bark of twigs in the canopy suggests that they may be quite numerous here.

In 2007, the results of a national survey suggested that the grey squirrel population in the midlands of Ireland may have begun to decline. This was a surprising suggestion at the time. While grey squirrel introductions had occasionally failed elsewhere, such a decline in range had not been recorded anywhere else that the species has established itself as an invasive population. In this report, the decline in grey squirrel range was anecdotally attributed, by foresters and gamekeepers, to an increase in range and numbers of the pine marten which is known to prey on squirrels. It is now thought that the red squirrel, which evolved alongside the pine marten, has learnt to avoid it while the recently introduced grey squirrel does not have this behaviour and is more susceptible to predation.

In 2009 Emma Sheehy of NUI Galway started a
study investigating the role of the pine marten in red
and grey squirrel population dynamics in Ireland.
First, she examined the distribution of these species in
counties Laois and Offaly in the midlands, where this
phenomenon had been reported, and also in County
Wicklow, where all three species were also present but
the grey squirrel range was not suspected to have gone
into decline. She found that the grey squirrel was not
doing well at all in many of the midland counties which
had seen a dramatic decline in recent years.

Squirrel numbers fluctuate annually in relation to
the previous year's autumn crop of tree seeds and winter
temperature, and it is normal to have good years and
bad years. But what Sheehy discovered was far beyond
what would be expected during normal population
fluctuations. She found that red squirrels were doing
very well in Laois, Offaly and in North Tipperary as a
consequence of the sustained reduction in grey squirrel
numbers and range. They had also started recolonising
parts of counties Longford, Westmeath, north Kilkenny
and Kildare. Considering that red squirrels had been
absent from much of the midland region for several
decades, and grey squirrels had once been abundant

as far west as the River Shannon, this new distribution was unexpected. However, grey squirrels continue to thrive in other parts of the country, including much of the east and the grey squirrel continues to expand into the south-west of Ireland.

If the pine marten is allowed to expand again it may bring with it a natural biological control of the invasive squirrel avoiding the need for artificial control measures and indirectly helping the survival of native woodlands. The pine marten provides a link between the woodlands of today and the forests inhabited by our ancestors. This summer, I am putting a custom-made breeding box for the pine martens high in a tree in the middle of our woodland. I want them to stay.

## Kite flying

As I approach the wood in the dawn light, a distinctive shape lifts off from the tallest tree. Long, pointed wings, a deeply forked tail and an overall red colour identifies it as a red kite. Harried by the local pair of hooded crows, it drifts lazily off across the fields, circling in the morning mist as it struggles to gain height. A red kite, like the familiar children's kite, seems to fly without any effort, gliding away on the updrafts and steering with its flexible tail. I have seen these exciting birds numerous times across Wicklow, but only recently in our own woodland. The red kite was once common across Britain and Ireland and there are even several Old Irish names for the species including *phreachain na gclearc* or *préachán ceirteach*. The latter name translates literally as 'cloth kite', referring to the birds' habit of decorating their nests with cloths and rags. But, like most of the predatory birds in Ireland, the red kite was persecuted and eventually wiped out here in the eighteenth century. Ned, the previous owner of our wood, never saw a red kite as they were long gone from Ireland when he farmed here in the late 1800s. These are inspirational birds whose decline and eventual extinction here mirrors the fortunes of our native woodlands.

In 2007 the Golden Eagle Trust launched an innovative project to reintroduce red kites to Ireland. The nearest surviving population was in the mountains of central Wales where they had hung on for centuries in the remote mountain valleys and woodlands. The decline of this remnant population began to change in the late twentieth century when numbers increased to over 1,000 pairs. So, it was to Wales that members of the Golden Eagle Trust (supported by the NPWS) went in search of a donor population that could be used to re-establish red kites in Wicklow, just eighty kilometres across the Irish Sea. Under licence and with the help of local ornithologists from the Welsh Kite Trust, they climbed numerous trees to seek out nests with three or more red kite chicks from which a single bird was removed before fledging. After veterinary clearance the young birds were rushed to their new homes and placed in release cages at a quiet location in the centre of Wicklow. Here they were reared with a minimum of human contact until the great day came when the doors of the cages were left open and these magnificent birds took to the Irish skies for the first time in over two centuries.

Wicklow was chosen for the first releases because it most closely resembled the landscape of Wales where the birds had managed to eke out an existence. This county is one of the most wooded in Ireland and has an intimate mix of lowland farmland habitats with plenty of hedgerow trees and small woodlands. From then on, annual releases of a total of 120 kites helped to supplement the population although not all the young birds survived. Some fell victim to illegal poisoning, shooting and collision with overhead wires. But the bulk of the released birds survived and fed successfully in their new home. Several territorial pairs formed and, in 2010, the news emerged of the first successful breeding with wild red kites fledging naturally from a nest in Ireland. In County Down a second release site had already been established by the RSPB in the rolling hills to the north of the Mourne Mountains and here another small population of red kites became slowly established.

Marc Ruddock, an experienced raptor biologist, was appointed by the Trust to monitor the Wicklow birds, follow their movements and oversee a third release of forty kites in the Fingal area of north Dublin. The landscape there contrasts starkly with Wicklow, consisting mainly of very large flat arable fields and much less woodland. In Wicklow, studies of the diet of the kites, based on prey remains in the nest, sensor cameras in the trees and regurgitated pellets, found a wide range of prey species. Crows, rabbits, rats and pigeons made up a sizeable proportion of the diet but, surprisingly, invertebrates (mainly insects) were present in a significant number of pellets. Like the buzzard, the red kite has a habit of feeding in ploughed fields where earthworms and insects are turned up by the plough. I have seen one pair following a tractor that was harrowing the soil.

All of the released kites and many wild nestlings were marked with large numbered wing tags which are often visible as the birds fly overhead. Radio-tracking of a sample of the birds showed that the younger kites wandered widely and were recorded throughout Ireland (north and south). There were also quite a few exchanges between the regional populations with pairs forming between birds from each area. Unfortunately, there were also plenty of mortalities recorded, the majority of these from poisoning.

The red kite is now well and truly re-established as a breeding bird in Ireland with three local populations and over a hundred pairs in the east of the country. So far, red kites in Ireland appear to be highly connected to the release areas with slow expansion in their breeding range. In winter the local population gathers in several communal night roosts. On a cold January evening I stood transfixed watching the spectacle of over fifty kites circling in the air and roosting in a group of trees near the Wicklow village of Avoca. A small number of birds are still killed each year by taking poison intended for foxes, crows and rats but they will be safe on our land and I look forward to the day when a nest is built in the wood.

## *Aging trees*

When I first started to explore our woodland, my attention was immediately drawn to the largest and, I presumed, oldest trees. The giant birch tree, lording it over the damp slopes, measures over a metre in diameter at chest height. It is surrounded by younger, middle-aged specimens which may have come from its seed. Hanging over the river, a number of old alders make the giant birch look quite slim by comparison. The largest alder here measures 1.6 metres across its waist. The age of these trees remains a mystery, but my guess is that they were saplings in the early nineteenth century, around the time that Napoleon was expanding his empire in Europe. They would have been mature by the time Ned and his family worked in our woodland in the late 1800s.

The science of aging trees has its own name: dendro-chronology. This uses various techniques for dating events, environmental change and archaeological artefacts by examining the characteristic patterns of annual growth rings in tree trunks. Any freshly cut tree stump shows a series of concentric rings circling the heartwood and fanning out towards the bark on the edge. Naturally, the outer rings represent the youngest growth years of the tree but not all the rings are uniform

– some are thinner, some thicker, some light and some dark. Trees add two new layers to their diameter each year. The first, added in spring, is lighter in colour, has the larger cells and grows fast. In summer, as available moisture becomes scarce, growth generally slows down and the wood has smaller, darker cells. Deciduous trees, which lose their leaves in the autumn, do not grow any further in the winter so two alternating bands of light and dark wood in the rings represent a full year's growth.

The thickness of each ring or band results from growth patterns that reflect the conditions of that season or the year. A warm, wet summer may cause more cellulose to be added giving a wider band. A year in which there was an outbreak of insect damage to the foliage or when a tree was affected by disease may be represented by a narrow ring indicating poor growth. This produces a unique 'bar code' for each tree which can be matched against similar patterns in other trees of known age. Where the trees have been managed, for example by coppicing or pollarding, a much narrower ring results in the year of cutting so cycles of past management can be identified from the width of the rings.

I remember visiting the Natural History Museum in London which houses a cross section of the trunk of a giant sequoia tree showing nearly 1,800 years of growth rings. The specimen has been in the Museum since 1893, after the tree was felled in California, so the tree started growing in the first century AD. The rings are labelled with notable events in history such as the Great Fire of London and the Battle of Waterloo. A tree does not have to die or be felled for the rings to be examined as scientists often take a thin core by drilling into the centre and extracting a long, pencil-width sample of the rings which can then be examined under the microscope.

Dendrochronology also uses other techniques such as radiocarbon dating where the amount of carbon-14 isotope in the timber is compared against tree ring data. It is always calibrated against other organic material of known age and this allows scientists to work out the exact date that a tree started to grow or the year that a particular ring was laid down inside the living organism. This technique has often been used to date the 'bog oak' logs that are extracted from Ireland's peatlands or archaeological finds made of wood from ancient periods such as the Bronze Age.

As well as the great age of the venerable trees in our woodland, I have always been impressed by their massive height and bulk. To appreciate this fully I sometimes lie prostrate on the ground beneath the giant birch and stare up into the crown, marvelling at the strength of the branches and the intricate patterns of twigs and leaves high above.

I had a look through the Tree Register of Ireland to find the tallest, widest or oldest recorded specimens on this island. The surviving native species are no match in height for the introduced conifers which fill all top ten places, led by a specimen coast Douglas fir in Avondale Forest Park, County Wicklow, measured at 61 metres high. Widest girth is also dominated by introduced conifers, but the King Oak at Charleville Estate, County Offaly, makes fifth place at 8.5 metres around its main trunk. Many of the branches of this pedunculate oak now rest on the ground and it has been aged at up to 500 years.

Conifers were not always the largest trees in Ireland. In the National Museum of Ireland, an impressive dug-out canoe, known as the Lurgan Boat and dated from the Bronze Age, measures nearly fifteen metres in length. Carved from a single straight trunk of oak, the original tree may have stood up to thirty metres from the ground to the highest leaf, or about the height of a modern ten-storey building. Transforming a massive oak tree into this sleek canoe, using just stone axes and fire, must have taken our prehistoric ancestors some years to complete. Discovered in County Galway in 1901, it took nearly a month to transport the canoe from Lurgan bog to Milltown railway station. When it finally arrived by rail in Dublin, the boat was pulled through the streets on specially linked, horse-drawn carts to the gates of the National Museum.

### Requiem for the ash

I am starting to notice that some of the ash trees in our wood are in trouble. Their upper branches are bare except for the ragged remains of last year's ash keys. I have also noticed some small ash saplings where the leader has died off and the tree has put out a new shoot in an attempt to survive. Could this be the beginning of changes brought about by global warming? The first ash trees here to be affected by this problem, known as ash dieback, are on the edges of the wood but pictures of the canopy taken from a drone indicate that some of the trees in the centre are also starting to show signs of sickness.

Ash dieback is a serious disease caused by the fungal pathogen *Hymenoscyphus fraxineus*. The spores of the fungus blow in the wind and infect ash foliage turning the leaf-tips brown. It damages the leaves and twigs by making a chemical that is very toxic to the ash.[79] The fungus produces spores which form sticky masses and may then spread through the leaf stalks, down into the branches, trunk and roots, blocking off the tree's water supply. The leaves wilt and turn brown, lesions appear on the trunk and twigs decay resulting in crown dieback. In desperation the wounded tree can produce excessive side shoots on the trunk even as the bark turns a sick-looking brown or orange. The fungus then forms its spores in the leaf litter under the tree and these are dispersed in the wind. The spores can only survive in the air for a few days so dispersal is limited. Even so, the disease has spread rapidly across much of Europe. It was first noted in Ireland in October 2012 on plants imported from continental Europe and is now recorded in every county. The disease can affect ash trees of any age and in any setting. It can be fatal, particularly among younger trees, while older specimens can hang on a bit longer as they have greater resources at their disposal.

I am grieving already for these fine trees with their smooth, white bark and beautiful pinnate leaves. While

I will mourn the loss of ash in our woodland it will also be interesting to see what species takes their place as gaps open up in the canopy. Ash is so common in the landscape that it will have dramatic effects across the country once the disease really takes hold. Almost every hedgerow has some ash and, along with hawthorn, it must be one of the most abundant woody plants in Ireland. The Irish name for our local village is *Áth na Fuinseoge* (Ashford, or ford of the ashes) and there are numerous other examples around the country, such as Lough Fermanagh (lake of the ash) in County Roscommon. History tells us that ash trees were often grown in important locations of Ireland. The historic kingship of *Usnagh* had an ash at its centre. Another one, known as *Bile Tortan,* stood in County Meath roughly at the centre of a triangle formed by the three sacred places of *Tara, Tlaghtga* and *Tailltiu.* This was regarded in Celtic times as a protection by the gods of the land and its fertility.[80]

Pure ashwoods are relatively rare in Ireland. Much more common are mixtures of ash with many other species. I have been in one woodland that clings onto limestone cliffs in the heart of County Fermanagh where ash was the dominant species and another one at Slieve

Carron in the Burren region of County Clare. As there is normally plenty of sunlight penetrating the canopy of small leaves, the shrub, field and ground layers of vegetation below are often well developed. Both oak and ash come into leaf quite late in the spring so there can be a flush of woodland plants such as wood anemone and lesser celandine before the shade from the canopy closes in. The appearance of new leaves on the trees is often regarded in rural areas as a sign of the summer to come. 'Oak before ash, we're in for a splash; ash before oak we're in for a soak' was a traditional country saying that I learnt in childhood.

In limestone landscapes like the Burren, the ash trees are often stunted in growth due to the thin soils. Base-rich woods with a large amount of ash can be especially important for molluscs which need calcium for their shells and ancient upland ashwoods include some special insect species. Another feature is the local presence of base-rich groundwater seepages and springs where the invertebrate fauna can include a number of rare species such as caddisflies. Apart from the dieback disease, other threats to ashwoods include overgrazing by sheep and rabbits in the western and northern uplands and expansion of deer populations everywhere leading to change in the woodland structure, ground flora impoverishment and difficulties for regeneration. The loss of ash trees is likely to lead to replacement by sycamore and other species which are generally not native in Ireland resulting in changes to the composition of the woods.

I wonder if there is any hope for ash trees in view of the rapid spread of the disease. Is there a resistant strain of the species that will survive the initial onslaught to pass on its genes to the next generation? The UK Forest Research Agency began a project in 2013 to identify inherent resistance in ash trees from a range of locations across Britain, Ireland and the mainland of Europe. Seed was collected from fourteen different sites to ensure that there was some genetic diversity. Around 155,000 trees were planted and subsequently monitored for signs of infection, tolerance and survival over a five-year period. First-year survival was about 96 per cent but, by the end of five years, over ninety per cent of the trees showed signs of infection while some were infected but still alive. From the few apparently tolerant trees, thousands of cuttings were taken and grafted onto new ash root stock. These were then planted out and monitored for continued survival. However, it could be

12 to 15 years before these grafted trees begin to flower and up to twenty years before they set seed, so it may be a long wait until we have some resistant nursery stock. The recent COVID-19 emergency in the world's human population has taught us a lot about what a pandemic can do.

We know that there is wide genetic diversity among populations of ash and it is hoped that finding the strains that are resistant to the pathogen will allow propagation of future healthy ash trees from these. Scientists from the University of Copenhagen in Denmark, where the disease is well established, have identified DNA markers in ash which appear to be tolerant to the fungus causing ash dieback. I will be watching our ash trees closely over the next few years to see if there is any inherent resistance here. In a woodland such as ours, where biodiversity is more important than timber production, we will be leaving nature to take its course and it will become apparent quite soon which, if any, of the ash trees are tolerant of the disease.

Whatever happens in the future it is certain that some plants and animals associated with ash will suffer at least in the short term. Recent research in the UK has produced the most comprehensive account of all plant and animal species known to use ash. A staggering total of nearly a thousand species were listed. The most diverse group was the lichens with 548 species. Obligate species – those found only on ash and not on other trees – numbered forty-five species, mainly invertebrates such as the ash flower gall mite and ash sawfly.[81] However, some of the main group of species using ash are also found on other trees and presumably they will come to depend more on these. If the dieback is slow, then perhaps the gaps in the canopy of many poorly managed woodlands will help them to diversify by allowing sunlight to reach the forest floor, thus stimulating seedlings to germinate. I am optimistic that nature will find a way around this as it has with many other plant pathogens.

### Forest bathing

Diseases in trees may be exacerbated by the stress of climate breakdown. As well as threatening biodiversity, stresses caused by modern civilisation can also take their toll on individual people. A friend rings me to ask if she can use our woodland for some forest bathing. This is an increasingly popular activity, also called forest therapy, which does not involve getting wet but simply offers an opportunity for people to take time out, slow down and connect with nature. In Japan, the practice is decades old and known as *shinrin-yoku*, which means 'taking in the forest'. Although people have been taking walks in the country's forests for centuries, new studies show that such activity could have benefits for both our mental and physical wellbeing. As more research highlighted the benefits of *shinrin-yoku*, the Japanese government incorporated it into the country's health programme. In South Korea this type of nature therapy is a structured part of the state welfare system for all citizens from childhood to old age.

A bathing session for a group can last several hours. The leader or instructor tries to hold people's attention in the present moment, to practice mindfulness and give their bodies and minds a chance to slow down. They move very slowly, touching the trees, looking at colours and patterns, and breathing deeply. Normally a looped trail, not more than two or three kilometres long, is used and paths close to flowing water are preferred. Participants often finish by sitting or lying down under trees and looking up through the branches. Shades of green and blue, the colours of the forest and the sky, are relaxing and looking at nature's patterns helps to stop thoughts spinning in the head.

There is now a very large and growing literature evidencing the links between the natural environment and people's general health and wellbeing. Research conducted by forest medicine expert Dr Qing Li has suggested that spending time around trees (or just filling the home with house plants, or vaporising tree essential oils) can reduce blood pressure, lessen stress, raise energy levels, boost the immune system and even help people lose weight.[82] However, some scientists believe that evidence for the outcomes of mindfulness practice in outdoor settings is very limited. Published assessments, it is claimed, are mostly clinical in approach and tend not to assess and evaluate outcomes at a more holistic level.[83] On a more general level, the eminent ecologist E.O. Wilson postulated that humans are 'hard-wired' through evolution to hold an emotional and psychological attachment to nature. In a largely industrialised society, we spend increasing proportions of our lives indoors which disrupts our connection with nature and can lead to negative impacts on wellbeing.

I spoke to Shirley Gleeson who is a certified Forest Therapy Guide, Mentor and Trainer with the European

Forest Therapy Institute and I asked her what ecotherapy involves. She helps people practice mindfulness, focusing all the senses on nature around them. Regular forest bathers learn to listen to simple things like the wind in the leaves, feel the texture of bark and notice the patches of sunlight on the forest floor. She quotes research from the University of Derby which identifies five pathways to a connection with nature. These include beauty, meaning, compassion, senses and emotions. Ultimately, developing a caring attitude towards nature must lead any individual to understand and support the need for conservation. People who undertake this transformation begin to see forests and other natural habitats in a different way. They start to integrate nature into their everyday lives and to see their own difficulties in the context of a much wider world.

As an ecologist, I am used to looking at woodland as a functioning system of plants and animals interacting with each other and their environment. But I am beginning to see and appreciate how such places can also help us in our daily lives by providing a break from the pressurised society in which we live. As I enter the woodland it wraps itself around me, blocking out views and sounds in the rest of the landscape. I feel a sense of belonging in our own woodland as I walk its familiar paths, checking little details like the new leaves on the trees or the louder sound of the river after a night of rain. Thoughts are more focused on this time and place and less on what is happening elsewhere or in the past and future. After even a few minutes of woodland bathing I feel refreshed and ready for the next challenge.

## Autumn – Fruits of the forest

In autumn the oak trees along the road drop their acorns and the leaves start to turn many shades of brown. But things were not always so predictable for the owners of the land a century ago. In the autumn of 1914, Ned and Sarah's eldest daughter Jane contracted tuberculosis and died. A year later another tragedy struck the family. Ned's youngest son Dan was a forest worker employed by the estate to harvest timber in the Devil's Glen. He also managed the woodland on his family's land by coppicing alder and hazel trees to produce a steady supply of useful fencing posts, building spars and firewood. But he was restless for adventure so, accompanied by a friend from the neighbouring townland, he ran off to join the British Army. By 1915, Europe was

engulfed by the Great War and Dan was sent to France
with his regiment. Just three weeks later he was killed
in action but it would be several more weeks before his
family received the terrible news by telegram.

His father, now in his seventies and becoming frail,
never recovered from the shock of Dan's death and he
died a year later. Ned's widow Sarah moved to Dublin
to live with one of her married daughters and her eldest
son, William, inherited the family farm. He now burnt
coal in the stove and he had no interest in the woodland.
It became neglected, except when a sheep went missing
and William would search among the trees only to find
it caught in the brambles that filled the woodland floor.

I have a love–hate relationship with brambles. I love
nothing better than foraging for juicy blackberries in the
September sunshine. It reminds me of carefree childhood
days when I raced my siblings to fill the biggest pot.
Ireland's much-loved poet Seamus Heaney captured the
joy of the traditional blackberry picking in his country
childhood.

> Late August, given heavy rain and sun
> For a full week, the blackberries would ripen.
> At first, just one, a glossy purple clot

Among others, red, green, hard as a knot.
You ate that first one and its flesh was sweet
Like thickened wine: summer's blood was in it
Leaving stains upon the tongue and lust for
Picking. Then red ones inked up and that hunger
Sent us out with milk cans, pea tins, jam-pots
Where briars scratched and wet grass bleached our
boots.

I hate the damn thorns on the briars that stretch out from the woodland jungle and continually block the paths. I have lost count of the number of times I have been snagged while trying to work on a woodpile. The bramble *Rubus fruticosus* is actually an aggregate of more than eighty different micro-species with stunning variation. This is because brambles may also reproduce by asexual means. As a result, all but a few botanical experts treat this large group as a single species. As I pluck the juicy berries to sweeten my porridge, I am aware that some of the micro-species have larger fruits or a sweeter taste and some ripen earlier than others. I have come to know the secret places along the woodland paths where I can be sure of a sweet treat. I am not the only forager here as blackbirds gorge themselves and foxes select the low-hanging fruit and leave seed-filled droppings on the path.

At the far end of the woodland is a stand of black-thorn, just as impenetrable as a clump of brambles. However, this is a woody shrub that can grow to the height of a small tree. Its thorns are sharp and the branches intertwine so it makes an ideal livestock barrier in a hedgerow. Blackthorn walking sticks are still quite popular and the timber was often used in the past to make crude weapons such as shillelaghs and cudgels. Like the bramble, blackthorn has a tempting juicy fruit called sloe that is a wild relative of the domes-ticated plums and cherries in the genus *Prunus*. I have a naturally sweet tooth and cannot manage to eat even one of these bitter, acidic fruits no matter how tempting they look. The old herbalists knew that sloes are strongly astringent although they must have been used over the millennia as the stones have been excavated from the cesspits of Dublin's Viking town. Today they can be used to flavour gin and make a fruity wine but both require large quantities of sugar.

If blackthorn is the queen of the hedgerow plants then the king is the hawthorn, also known locally as whitethorn or maybush because of its luscious sprays of white blossom in May. It doesn't flower well in our woodland as it is fairly intolerant of shade but the white flowers do shine in the early summer sunshine on the woodland edge. Then in September these turn magically into hanging bunches of dark red berries called haws. Flocks of thrushes, including the winter visitors, redwings and fieldfares, devour the berries. When the weather turns cold, haws may be present one day and gone the next. Although the fruits are hard and not very sweet, they were probably used as a food source by people in ancient Ireland. Some today make haw jelly or mix it with other wild fruits to make 'hedgerow jam'.[84] Back in eighteenth-century Dublin, poor citizens ground the abundant haws to meal and used them as a substitute for flour which they could ill afford.[85] I have heard tales of country children picking the buds and leaves of hawthorn on their way to school as they make a nice snack which was known as 'bread-and-cheese'. Hawthorn is endowed with magical qualities and isolated trees are often left untouched in the middle of a field as it is considered unlucky to damage a 'fairy tree'. There are many other traditional beliefs surrounding hawthorn in rural Ireland, some of which still survive today.

In September, the white blossoms of another woodland tree, the elder, turn over and mature into bunches
of luscious elderberries. We add the flowers to water
giving a very distinctive flavour to a refreshing cordial.
This type of 'elderflower champagne' is also quite widely
available now in cafés and restaurants. Beware the
potent purple dye that is released when you handle the
ripe fruit. Apparently, the Romans used elderberries as a
hair dye and in Ireland it was said that dark hair washed
with elderberries takes on rich, glossy shine.[86]

Holly is one of the most abundant trees in our
woodland but I now recognise that the dense shade cast
by its evergreen leaves is one of the reasons why there
has been poor regeneration in the past. It, in turn, is
shade tolerant hence its ability to regenerate so freely.
However, a positive benefit of the holly is its crop of
bright red berries that brighten up the dull colours of
the woodland but which only grow on female trees. The
fruit provides winter birds with welcome food when
other supplies are running low but the bitter taste and
toxic compounds in the berries make them unattractive
as human food. Luckily, I am not left hungry as the
apple and pear trees in the orchard are groaning with
fruit at this time.

## Woodland foraging

With my daughter Hazel, I am on one of our many autumn foraging trips in the Wicklow woodlands. Meticulously searching the ground under the trees, we find penny buns (ceps or porcini) and many other boletus fungi which we have come to regard as a delicacy in recent years. Other collectors have been here before us. The new multicultural nature of this country has made fungal foraging popular in Ireland, helped in part by the fashion of using wild foods in some of the smartest Irish restaurants. There are plenty of recipes for woodland species in the book *Forest Fungi in Ireland*, written jointly by mycologist Paul Dowding and chef Louis Smith.[87] My own interest in wild foods was stimulated many years ago by the book *Food for Free* in which the English naturalist Richard Mabey wrote about the foods to be found in the countryside.[88]

Foraging in the wild has always been part of life here since the Mesolithic period thousands of years ago when the country was occupied by hunter-gatherers and farming had not yet arrived in Ireland. As well as foraging for wild fruits, nuts, seeds, leaves and roots, these early people also hunted for wild game and fish. Most easily captured were small mammals like hares, fish such as eels and salmon and wild birds like ducks. Occasionally larger animals like wild pigs or red deer would have been trapped or killed with primitive weapons. The prevalence of wild mammal remains in the excavation of prehistoric settlements is testament to this.[89] Wild venison has a distinctive and delicious flavour. In the Wicklow woodlands deer are still very common today and, in the absence of large natural predators, the deer populations need to be controlled. But the level of hunting is far too low and the market for venison is poor.

For most of the Irish population today, there is still resistance to foraging or hunting for wild food as most people have grown up without the basic skills, are disconnected from nature or have no experience of eating anything other than convenience foods from a supermarket. Foraging is also associated with a more primitive lifestyle and with the starving population of the 1840s when the potato crop repeatedly failed leading to widespread famine and mass emigration.

The writer John Lewis-Stempel lived for a year on wild food only, gathered or hunted on his own farm. Much of his time was devoted to stalking small game such as rabbits, pigeons, ducks and pheasants. He was often hungry and, in his book *The Wild Life*, he admits that he had misjudged the sheer amount of work that was necessary to live in this way. 'Once you have picked or dispatched your food you will have to prepare it. Every time.'[90] This type of work is unfamiliar to most people today but we may need to relearn it in future as we begin to transform our lifestyles to meet the challenges of climate breakdown.

The recent upsurge in foraging in Ireland is mainly targeting plant food. Scientists have recognised the value of this in making a case for conservation by writing guides for the general reader. Peter Wyse Jackson produced an encyclopaedic volume entitled *Ireland's Generous Nature* which details all the wild plants useful for everything from food and medicine to building and basketry.[91] In their book *The Wild Food Plants of Ireland*, authors Tom Curtis and Paul Whelan focused more closely on wild crop relatives which are the genetic ancestors of all the food plants essential to both humans and domestic animals.[92] Selective breeding of these species over thousands of years has produced all the cultivated vegetables, fruit, crops and fodder plants that we use today. For example, the native wild cherry tree, which grows in woodland, hedgerows and scrub throughout the country, is the species from which the cultivars of sweet cherries were bred. Although there are wild cherry trees in our own woodland and hedges, I have never found any fruit beneath them and I suspect that the birds remove most of the cherries from the canopy before they fall.

To learn more about woodland foraging I met up with my friend Courtney Tyler, of Hips and Haws Wildcrafts, who runs a number of woodland-based courses. Together with Lucy O'Hagan of Wild Awake she runs an autumn course each year called 'Feasting with the Ancestors'. They invite participants to enjoy a weekend in the woods foraging for plants and fungi, culminating in a local wild feast. This provides a space to unwind, connect with nature and learn more about wild foods. Courtney emphasises that people need to learn not only identification and preparation skills but also the seasonality of certain wild foods. She remembers that her initial interest in foraging came from reading in summer whereupon she decided to go out and harvest the fleshy leaves of wild garlic that grow in great profusion in some Wicklow woods. Initially she was disappointed to find that they were only present for a short time in spring. So, she learnt to be there as soon as the first new shoots appeared in March or April to harvest the pungent leaves in quantity so that she could preserve them to use throughout the year. When covered with salt, the garlic loses a lot of moisture but keeps its fresh flavour. By crushing or blending the leaves with salt it becomes a thick green paste for use as a stock to flavour soups. If the proportion of salt is under six per cent the garlic ferments and keeps its really fresh flavours for up to a year. Sometimes she will mix the garlic leaves with other wild greens such as nettles, dandelions and hedge mustard which are emerging at the woodland edge at the same time. Courtney also dries the wild garlic leaves to add them with elderberries later in the year to a venison stew.

During summer the flowers of elder and primrose can be used to make herbal teas. According to Cyril and Kit O'Cleirin, the youngest leaves of hawthorn were used with speedwell to make a tea in medieval times at Holy Cross Abbey in County Tipperary.[93] Healthy drinks such as rosehip syrup, elderflower and gorse-flower cordial all help digestion.

Autumn is the time of abundance of fungi, nuts and berries. Most commercial hazelnuts are harvested from cultivated trees known as cobs. The native nuts are smaller but can be picked in large quantities when they're ripe and the shelled nuts make a tasty nibble to munch on while I'm out walking in the woods. If I manage to collect enough, I will roast the shelled nuts in the oven or use them to make hazelnut butter. Acorns also have many uses despite the high levels of tannin that they contain. They are collected from the ground beneath the trees and then 'leached' to remove the tannin. Cold leaching can be done by putting them in a cloth bag and immersing the bag in a clean stream where the water flushes them out over a day or two. Hot leaching is done by boiling the acorns a few times in a large pot. Courtney usually peels the acorns first and after leaching they are crushed, dried and ground into an acorn powder to make acorn pancakes or toasted to make acorn coffee. It has a really earthy flavour.

Burdock root is one of Courtney's favourite finds on the grassy edges of paths and glades in woodlands. She says 'it is delicious and nutritious but digging it is a huge job as the roots are massive. It makes a tasty base for soup stocks with a rich depth of flavour and is so good for you as a blood tonic.' She also digs up dandelion root which is roasted and blended with medicinal mush-rooms to make a dark, bitter but delicious coffee. When she first started discovering the benefits of dandelion, Courtney tried to make as many things as possible from that plant including vinegars and salts, salves, creams and lotions, dandelion flower pancakes, dandelion wine and everything she could think of with this common plant.

Foraging courses are growing in popularity, helping participants to find and identify wild leaves, flowers, fruits, nuts and fungi that are not only delicious but a bit of a curiosity in an otherwise predictable diet. Learning how to preserve these foods for the winter months is also a regular part of such courses and fermenting is coming back into fashion after hundreds of years. Courtney says that people she meets on her courses are 'intrigued to reconnect with some of the skills and knowledge about nature that we used to have'. However, she acknowledges that some people are against foraging because they fear the damage that this might do to vulnerable species and habitats. Her own view is opposite of this. She notes,

the more people connect with nature and feel a sense of ownership, the more likely they are to support nature conservation. Once people begin

to forage sustainably, they become more aware of
how scarce and localised some plants and animals
actually are and will be more likely to value them.

As Richard Mabey says in *Food for Free*, 'no one is
going to stand by while the hedge which provides his
sloe gin is bulldozed down'.

## Forest pharmacy

For most of recorded history, Irish people found the
remedies for common ailments in the fields, hedges and
woods of their own landscape. The ingredients were not
usually written down but were passed verbally from
generation to generation and often enlivened with a
dollop of magic or fairy lore. In recent times, herbal
medicine has come back into favour as people search
for an alternative to the pervasive pharmaceutical drugs
upon which our society has become so dependent.

This medicinal use of wild plants has been called
'nature's medicine chest' by the botanist Peter Wyse
Jackson. He stresses that, over past centuries, 'medicinal
plants have been used in Ireland to treat such a remarkable range of ailments, conditions, diseases and illnesses
that the list reads like a lexicon of human health care'.[94]

In fact, many of the early Irish botanical writings were largely produced to guide the medicinal use of plants by herbalists. The use of wild plants for traditional cures survived into the early twentieth century in some rural areas but the supposed magical properties of the plants often required accompanying rituals, such as rhymes or prayers, to be effective. Birch bark was used medicinally to treat eczema. The ash from burnt hazel was used to treat burns and bark was applied to cuts. Various parts of the ash tree (sap, bark, leaves, buds) were used in Ireland to treat ailments such as fevers, warts, heartburn, ringworm, burns and earache. The leaves were used either fresh or boiled for rheumatism and gout. Wild garlic was extensively used for a wide range of ailments including severe rheumatism and sciatica where the sufferer was submerged in a bath containing boiled garlic.[95] These practices were gradually overtaken by conventional medicine, but even this was often based on wild plants such as the extraction of salicylic acid (aspirin) from the leaves of willow trees.

Among Ireland's best-known herbalist healers was Biddy Early who lived in nineteenth century County Clare. Her cures involved the use of such plants as nettles, cabbage, water cress and flax. Peter Wyse

Jackson visited her ruined cottage where he found twenty-two species of plants with recorded medicinal uses growing in the dark woodland surrounding the now roofless house. Among these was square-stalked elder, St John's wort, arum lily and wild angelica.

Even in cities such as Cork there were herb markets where medicinal plants were sold. There are still herbalists today who use wild woodland plants to alleviate various ailments. The loss of most of Ireland's wildwoods in past millennia removed an important reservoir of herbal remedies but also accelerated the decline of folk knowledge about the value of many plants for health.

### Woodland losses in recent centuries

Eileen McCracken was one of the key chroniclers of the sad story of woodland loss. This is one of the best examples of historical research used to track ecological changes in Ireland. McCracken began her classic book with the statement that

> In 1600 about one-eighth of Ireland was forested; by 1800 the proportion had been reduced to a fiftieth as a result of the commercial exploitation of the

Irish woodlands following on the establishment of English control over the whole country.[96]

This long-held view that the settlers, planted by the English monarchy, bore full responsibility for the clearance of the native woodlands of Ireland was challenged by Oliver Rackham of Cambridge University. He argued that the Irish woodlands had already been much reduced in earlier times. The Civil Survey of Ireland in 1654–56 was the equivalent of the Domesday Book in England. It recorded many thousands of woods and Rackham has calculated from these records, combined with sources studied by McCracken, that only 2.1 per cent of Ireland was covered by woodland in the mid-seventeenth century. This would make Ireland only one-third as wooded as England at the same time. Unlike the neighbouring island, where woodland husbandry was already well established, Irish forests may well have been in a neglected state.[97] It is clear that very little, if any, of the primaeval forests had survived earlier exploitations and that most of the woods were of secondary growth.

Using a combination of documentary sources and pollen records can be the most accurate way of dating the final removal of the forests. In Killarney, for example, there are numerous references from the sixteenth and seventeenth centuries to felling the more accessible woodlands for charcoal production, oak bark for tanning and timber for barrel-making and shipbuilding. Pollen records confirm that there were significant falls in tree pollen in the seventeenth century. By contrast, in the north-east, the pollen record and written history seem to be at odds with each other. In County Down the documentary evidence of Jacobean forest exploitation is not supported by the pollen record which does not show dramatic falls in tree pollen. Instead, it suggests a gradual reduction in tree cover over at least a thousand years. There is nothing found so far that suggests an acceleration of this trend in the seventeenth century. The picture that emerges instead is of less abundant large forest trees which were replaced by hazel scrub. The Burren of north Clare, at this time, was still largely covered by hazel and other trees such as birch, elm, oak and yew, which were once more common in this landscape. Pollen studies as well as documentary sources suggest that the hazel was much reduced in the nineteenth century as the human population rose.[98]

McCracken discussed the traditional view that large tracts of woodland were cut in the early seventeenth century to destroy the cover for the displaced Irish who had retreated into the woods. Although there are plenty of documentary records of such propositions, the evidence for this actually taking place is meagre, according to McCracken.

In 1399, when McMorough, King of Ireland, lay in hiding with 3,000 men in the woods, west of Kilkenny, King Richard II ordered the mobilisation of 2,500 men to cut down the wood and burn the trees. In 1585, Perrott suggested that the Munster woods should be cut 'to deprive the rebels of their places of succour' and he alleged that there were Englishmen willing to undertake the task if the government would lend them £5,000 for three years. The term 'woodkerne' was commonly applied by officialdom in the sixteenth and seventeenth centuries to the displaced Irish people that lived in the woods. They were clearly feared and categorised with wild animals as sub-human. Blennerhasset in 1610 described the wolf and woodkerne as the most serious dangers to the Ulster colonists and recommended periodic manhunts to track down the human wolves to their lairs. A proclamation of 1660 offered rewards of £3 to £10 for the betrayal of 'a tory or woodkerne'. William Stewart of Newtownstewart, County Tyrone, wrote in 1683, 'the gentlemen of the country have been so hearty in that chase that of thirteen in the county where I live, in November the last was killed two days before I left home'.

McCracken found many documented examples of seventeenth-century leases that required tenants to clear timber annually in order to develop the farmland on the estates. An example from the 1670s was the Brownlow estate in Lurgan, County Armagh, where the landlord wished to clear scrub only and to preserve the good timber. On this estate, leases required the tenants to 'plant orchards and set ditches with hawthorn and saplings of ash, oak, hazel and sycamore 30 feet apart'. It has to be remembered that, in the seventeenth century, much of the country was devoid of hedgerows and was managed on the openfield or 'rundale' system. Enclosed fields were unknown and livestock were accompanied at all times by herdsmen or, more usually, by children. The clusters of dwellings were surrounded by 'gardens' where crops were grown and the outer fields were unfenced and grazed as common land. This practice survived in a few isolated places such as west Mayo and north Donegal into the twentieth century.

McCracken linked the final phase of woodland clearance in Ireland with the industrial uses of timber for charcoal production, manufacture of barrel staves and the export of quantities of wood for shipbuilding and house-building. Coopering, or the manufacture of barrels to hold everything from salted fish to beer, was a widespread industry up to the nineteenth century. The work of the cooper was to produce the two shapes of timber that were combined to make the wooden barrels. The curved planks or staves fitted perfectly together while the flat circular pieces were fitted to the top and bottom to form the complete barrel. Up to the early nineteenth century, the hoops which bound the staves together were made of hazel or willow which is very pliable. Later, iron hoops became common and these circles often survive in historic sites when the wooden barrels have completely rotted away.

The 1804 estate map that covers our own land in Wicklow marks the site of the woodland as 'furze'. While this is a local name for gorse it was often used in previous centuries to describe rough woodland such as that which may grow in wet areas. The landlord would later plant hundreds of thousands of new trees across the estate but may have overlooked this small corner of the valley allowing it to regenerate naturally as wildwood.

## The old estates

Old woodland reaching down to the shores of a lake makes an attractive view but also provides very special wildlife habitats which are relatively scarce in the country. I visited one such area at Crom Estate on the shores of Upper Lough Erne in County Fermanagh. The entrance to the estate is most impressive as the winding drive leads up to a towering castle that would not be out of place in a television series such as *Downton Abbey*. The original Crom Castle was built in 1610 during the Ulster Plantation but the present castle dates from the 1830s. Shan Bullock, a poet and novelist who grew up on the estate, remembered the big house as 'a world of lavish magnificence, of endless goings and comings and doings, a civilisation, a little state, splendid and stirring with life'.

The National Trust for Northern Ireland acquired the estate in 1987 but the castle itself continues in the ownership of the family of the Earl of Erne. The National Trust is best known across the UK for owning and managing large historic houses and gardens but it also has custodianship of significant areas of high nature value, including old estates and coastal properties. A key feature of the National Trust properties is that they are all open to the public and many provide interpretative materials that help members of the public to understand the need for nature conservation. The Crom Estate now has over 20,000 visitors each year; there is a visitor centre and café and plenty of good educational material that helps to explain the conservation objectives to the public.

One of the unique features of the Crom Estate is the intimate mix of lake and woodland. There are few other places in Ireland or Britain where the natural transition from open water, swamp, fen, wet grassland and wet woodland to mature broadleaf woodland is as well developed and occurs on such a large scale as at Crom. The ancient oak and ash woodlands and the many mature parkland trees are of particular importance. Together they comprise the largest block of semi-natural oak woodlands in Northern Ireland. Although the many fine stands of oak were planted here less than 200 years ago, experts agree that woodland has been present continually on this site for much longer. The ancient history of these woodlands is revealed in the frequency in the local place names containing the word Derry (from the Irish *doire* meaning oakwood).

I went there to meet Malachy Martin of the National Trust who has spent a number of years working at Crom but is now the Trust's Land and Nature Officer for the whole province. We walked through old woods where the leaves of the trees sparkled in the dappled sunlight. Enormous oak standards dominate the canopy, some with trunks of several metres around the base. These huge veterans are like an ecosystem in themselves with a hanging garden of ferns and mosses and hundreds of insect species that feed on their leaves and timber. Around them were stands of hazel that looked like former coppice. The estate is notable for its lichen and fungi species, some of which are found nowhere else in Northern Ireland, while a large number of rare or endangered plants also occur here, including greater water-parsnip, blue-eyed grass and bird's nest orchid.

Crom is also rich in insects with twelve species of dragonflies and damselflies recorded as well as rare moths and butterflies including the purple hairstreak and silver-washed fritillary. Among the breeding birds the garden warbler is a speciality which returns each year to the woodlands on the shores of the lake. All eight of Northern Ireland's bat species have been recorded roosting at Crom where the intimate mosaic of woodland and water provides ideal foraging during the summer.

Malachy explained that the level of Upper Lough Erne had been artificially altered on several occasions in the past, most recently in the 1950s, with the construction of a hydroelectric power station at Ballyshannon near the outlet to Donegal Bay. This created an open fringe around the drumlins which gradually filled with wet woodland of alder and willow. In the open areas this is managed as fen meadow or purple moor-grass and rush pasture. Unfortunately, the woodlands also contain the non-native rhododendron, laurel and sycamore which are removed on an ongoing basis. The introduced fallow deer are also a very big problem in the woodlands where their browsing can prevent trees regenerating. They also swim out to the islands so none of the woodlands are free from deer. They must be culled each year to control their populations. Deer fencing is also used in some areas to allow regeneration to get going. There are some huge parkland trees spread across the estate grasslands where former hedges have been removed.

According to Malachy, 'nature conservation management here is a balancing act between the needs of wildlife, historic landscapes, visitor access and the requirements of the donor family'. As an example, he explains,

> deadwood management can be one potential area of conflict. The poor dispersal abilities of saproxylic invertebrates [those that are dependent on dead or decaying wood] means that deadwood should ideally remain in situ. However, in specific areas of parkland, it may be desirable to remove deadwood in order to maintain the historic character or visual aesthetics. This is not removed off-site but stacked nearby but out of sight where it forms a new microhabitat.

In general, a policy of minimum intervention has been adopted with respect to managing the woodlands at Crom. The management plan specifies relatively simple and effective practices such as deer and goat management, removal of invasive non-native species, and ride and glade maintenance which are undertaken annually. Other issues such as regeneration, age structure and deadwood volumes are investigated, with more complex data collated in condition-monitoring reports.

The historical removal of old trees from native woodlands is a very complex subject, as this harvesting did not necessarily cause the loss of woodlands. In many cases where there was active management, including the felling of big trees, the woods actually survived through the centuries. Many of these woods were in private ownership and most still are.

Another ancient woodland that has been protected within an estate is at Charleville Castle on the edge of the town of Tullamore, County Offaly. The castle was built after the 1798 rebellion by Charles William Bury, Earl of Charleville, and is said to be the finest example of gothic-revival architecture in the country. The estate includes a small lake which is now overgrown with reeds and a stream runs along the western perimeter. The estate woodland is considered to be one of very few ancient woodlands remaining in Ireland, with some parts undisturbed for at least 200 years. The King Oak, close to the front gate, is the most famous tree on the estate. Nobody is quite sure of its age but some estimates place it between 500 and 700 years. A stand of old oaks near the castle was felled in 1962 and ring counts suggested they were mostly planted in the seventeenth century with the oldest dated to 1490.[99] The present woodland has a varied age structure and is relatively intact with areas of both closed and open canopy and regenerating saplings present in the latter.

I paid a visit to Charleville Castle to attend a meeting of woodland ecologists, foresters and other enthusiasts. With some time to spare before the meeting I set off to wander through the sun-filled woodland. Immediately, I could see that there were many large and impressive oak trees with their canopies well above the main woodland. Beneath them was a dense stand of young ash trees which are so closely spaced that they must have regenerated naturally. I found some young oak saplings near the entrance to the estate. But I also saw some laurel with its evergreen foliage casting dense shade on the ground below and preventing any seedlings from establishing where it grew.

At Charleville, approximately ten per cent of the woodland has been under-planted with conifers and other exotic trees, but the rest of the area is dominated by pedunculate oak with much ash and scattered wych elm. Birch grows well in the wetter soils on the estate. The shrub layer is composed largely of hazel, hawthorn and blackthorn. The ground layer is varied, including damp flushed slopes with wild garlic and drier, more open areas covered with moss. There are many species of fungi here and there is a large population of the rare whorl snail *Vertigo moulinsiana*. The site has benefitted from a Native Woodland Scheme a number of years ago and this area has been recently managed by forester Paddy Purser on behalf of the owner David Hutton Bury. His work involved tackling the overgrazing problem, deer fence repair, under-planting, felling of exotics, creating new deadwood habitat, replanting with native species of a previously felled conifer area, and control of rhododendron and cherry laurel. This old woodland requires very special care to ensure it survives the centuries ahead.

The walled estates are among the few places where old woodland survived in past centuries as the wealthy owners had the luxury of being able to preserve their grounds while much of Ireland's population was struggling to survive and poorer farmers needed to clear other native woodland for agriculture, building, firewood and many other uses. Well-managed woodlands can be a renewable resource providing a continual supply of useful materials. The consistency of ownership and long-term objectives of some estate owners helped to ensure that a few continuously wooded habitats remain within their boundaries to this day. Frequently, however, the management of these woods has lapsed as the number of estate staff dwindled. Some have become infested by invasive species such as rhododendron or damaged by excessive deer grazing while traditional practices such as coppicing have been abandoned. But there are a few examples now where these trends have been arrested and the value of maintaining woodland for future generations is recognised.

## Woodland nature reserves

Union Wood is located on a rocky outcrop on the eastern bank of the Ballysadare River, between the villages of Ballysadare and Collooney in County Sligo. Close by is Markree Castle, the ancestral seat of the Cooper family. The castle, which is partially moated by the River Unshin, is today a family-run hotel. I walked around the woodland with Tim Roderick, District Conservation Officer with the NPWS. He has worked for the Service for over twenty years so knows the business of conservation in some detail. Tim has a background in forest management so he is the ideal person to explain the conservation measures that are needed to manage this important remnant of the natural vegetation of the area.

Over half of the site comprises mixed woodland and conifer plantation. Almost 40 per cent of the woodland here consists of mature sessile oak, mixed with downy birch, holly and rowan. The ground flora is dominated by greater woodrush and is typical of acidic soils. The semi-natural parts of the wood are typical of a western oak wood. The site also contains a good range of sub-habitats, including deeper soils supporting ash and hazel woodland, streams, and pockets of damp woodland typified by remote sedge. The shrub and ground flora are somewhat diminished by deer grazing but localised areas support a rich diversity of bryophytes and herbaceous plants, such as enchanter's nightshade, pignut and violets. Hazel, hawthorn and blackthorn are also present in the shrub layer.

There are different theories about the origin of the woodland's name, but is thought that at least some of the woodland was planted to mark the Act of Union between Britain and Ireland in 1800. The presence of an area of wet and dry heath on the hilltop at Union Rock adds diversity to the site. The wood supports a range of mammals, including pine marten, badger, fox and red squirrel but it is also heavily grazed by a herd of fallow deer. Raven, kestrel and sparrowhawk

nest here and buzzards are a recent addition to the
raptors in the wood. One of these impressive birds
took off from the canopy as we passed by. Despite its
proximity to the town of Ballisodare, the woodland felt
wild with a canopy of oaks casting a dappled shade on
the vegetation below. The main uses of the site are for
commercial forestry and recreation. The woodland site
is a popular amenity area used for walking, horse riding,
scrambling/quad biking and occasional orienteering.
Deer hunting also takes place on a seasonal basis.

A conservation management plan for the site was
prepared for the period 2005–2010 but this has not yet
been updated to reflect the work carried out over many
years since then. As we walked, Tim explained that the
main restoration work began in 2004. One of the key
management actions has been the removal of exotic
conifers that were planted many years ago among the
native trees. Every few years forestry contractors are
engaged to sweep through the cleared areas and remove
any young conifer regrowth. Exotic rhododendron is
also a problem here and its large purple flowers were
very evident on my visit. The shrub covers approximately five hectares, a quarter of all the oak woodland.
This is more difficult to remove as it requires cutting

and treatment of the cut stumps. But the soil contains many seeds that germinate when the area is cleared and constant maintenance is needed to ensure that the plant does not spread again. Unfortunately, rhododendron is present on Coillte land surrounding the site and this provides a ready source of seed to affect the protected part of the woodland.

Deer grazing is also a serious problem for the growth of young trees and this has been tackled by the installation of many kilometres of deer fencing around the woodland. One-way deer leaps are incorporated to allow escape for any deer that do manage to get inside. Dead trees are left in situ within the woodland where the rotting timber provides an important habitat for insects and other invertebrates. To help in replacing native trees of local provenance the conservation plan proposed that NPWS would produce nursery stock from the site by collecting any available acorns during the few years when the seeds are produced by oaks. The plan also committed the NPWS to undertake long-term monitoring to determine the effectiveness of native woodland conversion by measurement of critical factors such as rhododendron clearance, native woodland regeneration and changes in the vegetation.

In some areas the oak trees form an even-aged
stand suggesting that historically parts of the woodland
were felled and replanted. Here the woodland canopy
is quite dense and would benefit from opening up to
allow light to reach the forest floor. But Tim Roderick
says that 'some people see tree-felling in a protected
area as a terrible thing to do'. He knows that this area
needs management to put right some of the misguided
treatment of the past and to improve it for wildlife.
Bracken has also become a problem for regeneration in
some areas. Tim believes that this could be tackled by
putting some pigs in to root up the stolons and stimulate
the seed sources in the soil but they would need to be
corralled with electric fencing to stop them wandering.

At the opposite end of the country lies another old
woodland nature reserve that sweeps right down to the
shores of Bantry Bay. It has a magical feel to it with
gnarled old oaks hanging low over a bubbling river
and winding stone steps leading up among the trees.
Glengarriff Wood became a nature reserve in the 1980s
when it was transferred from the Forest Service to the
Wildlife Service on the separation of these two state
bodies. This is a sizeable area of broadleaved woodland
comprised mainly of oak, holly, downy birch and rowan.

In common with the famous Killarney National Park, a little yew occurs here and strawberry tree is scattered through the woods. Although this is the site of an ancient woodland, it was also once part of an estate. Some of the present oak trees were probably planted here but it is thought there has been continuous woodland cover in at least parts of the valley for centuries.

At the beginning of the seventeenth century, the woodlands around Glengarriff were extensive, and it was from the shelter of these trees that O'Sullivan Bear set out with his followers early in 1602 on his long march to exile in Leitrim after the defeat of the Gaelic army at the Battle of Kinsale. In the first half of the eighteenth century, timber was coppiced to produce charcoal for the local iron smelter. In 1751 the woods became part of the estate of the White family, owners of Bantry House. They built a thatched hunting lodge in the middle of the woods, established a deer park and employed a gamekeeper. During the White's stewardship it seems the woods were largely protected from exploitation with contemporary records suggesting that the woods were never devastated to the extent that many other woods in Ireland were. The White family undertook some forestry planting. For example, Scots pine was planted in 1857 by the 2nd Earl of Bantry and a further seven hectares was planted later by the 4th Earl. Some of the Scots pine they planted can still be seen here today. Some exotic species such as beech, sycamore and rhododendron were also planted at that time.

I was introduced to Glengarriff Woods on a warm autumn day when a curtain of sea mist hung over the higher hills and the leaves dripped with moisture. My guide was Clare Heardman, the NPWS Conservation Ranger for this area. This is one of the classic Atlantic 'rainforests' which seems to be permanently wet. The branches of all the older trees are draped in deep mosses and hanging gardens of ferns and lichens. The invasive rhododendron is being systematically removed, with work initially being carried out by NPWS staff and, in latter years, with the help of the Native Woodland Scheme. Other areas within the woodland were planted in the past with conifers including Sitka spruce, lodgepole pine and western hemlock and these have subsequently been removed by Coillte. Fortunately, grazing pressure here from deer and livestock is low so natural regeneration with broadleaved trees is every-where to be seen. Young oak, rowan and birch trees spring from the mossy ground and even take root in crevasses in the rock. The frost-free Atlantic air and the humid atmosphere make an ideal place for propagation of these trees.

I came here partly to see the roost sites of the rare lesser horseshoe bat which have been found in three buildings in the woods. In the roof of a small stone-built house surrounded by trees, a special protected entry point in the roof has been constructed for the bats which like to fly straight in among the trees and do not like crossing open ground. What looks like a normal attic ladder through a trapdoor provides access for the roost to be checked and for NPWS staff to occasionally remove the deep deposits of bat droppings. The attic provides the very warm atmosphere needed by bats during the breeding season, where mother bats hang inside the roof space, carrying and protecting their young until they are big enough to fly and fend for themselves.

Bats have also been confirmed hibernating over winter in one of the buildings. To survive the colder months, they need steady temperatures of around five degrees centigrade and a damp atmosphere but such conditions are rarely found in buildings. So, Clare and her team designed and built a custom-made 'hibernacula' for the bats. Without her guidance I would never have found this amazing structure which is hidden beneath ferns and other hanging vegetation. Unlocking the steel door, we entered an artificial cave constructed from concrete box culverts that would normally be used to contain a stream flowing under a new road. The cool consistent atmosphere with water dripping from the ceiling provides the ideal conditions that the bats need to maintain their body functions in the winter torpor. It felt like the damp, dark basement of a long-forgotten house. Of course, there were no bats present at this time of year, but around 250 lesser horseshoe bats have roosted at the site in recent winters.

Glengarriff Wood is of international importance for both breeding and hibernating lesser horseshoe bats. Given the combination of winter, summer and foraging sites, this woodland nature reserve is one of the most important for the species in the south-west. There is also an important roost of approximately 100 long-eared bats within the woods. The insect prey that the rich woodland habitat supports is obviously important for the survival of these two sensitive mammal species. As Clare says, 'creating the conditions that allow the woodland and its special wildlife to regenerate by themselves is the key to management here'. This is a magical place which has managed to survive down through the centuries due to a benevolent ownership, informed management in recent years and a large slice of luck.

### Is rewilding feasible?

When I walk in our woodland it feels as if nature is controlling how it changes. I have to step over fallen trees and wind my way between trunks so close together that a wheelbarrow would not pass through. Ivy and honeysuckle climb all over the older trees and brambles continually try to close any paths that I make. What would happen, I wonder, if we simply walked away and did nothing to the woodland for fifty or a hundred years? Would some new, young trees grow in the gaps where their older relations had fallen? Would the river become blocked by fallen debris and change to a new course through the woodland? Would the habitat maintain its 'naturalness' here if there was no human disturbance or would deer grazing and invasive species compromise its future viability? Removing all human influence in order to allow natural processes to determine how an ecosystem develops has been recently popularised as 'rewilding', despite there being little hard evidence to show that it is feasible in Ireland.

Of course, nature is rarely allowed to take its own course without some form of human interference or 'management'. And there are even fewer examples where this process of natural succession and ecosystem change has been scientifically monitored. On the borders of England and Wales is a unique site called Lady Park Wood which was set aside as a 'natural' reserve for ecological research in 1944, and where the changes have been recorded in detail ever since. The succeeding 75 years of observations now represent one of the longest and most detailed records in Europe of how a woodland develops under the influence of natural factors.[100]

In this unique long-term study, trees and shrubs have been recorded at intervals, accumulating a detailed record of more than 20,000 individual beech, sessile oak, ash, wych elm, small-leaved lime, large-leaved lime, birch, hazel, yew and other species. In the seven decades since the study started, the wood has changed; trees grew, died and regenerated, and drought, disease and other events shaped its destiny. The volumes of dead wood have accumulated with many fallen logs and standing snags while the overall structure has become mature, varied and multi-layered. In other words, it looks and feels very natural. Each tree and shrub species has reacted in its own way to changes in the wood as a whole and to changes in the fortunes of its neighbours. Meanwhile, the wild fauna, flora and fungi have also responded, leaving the wood richer in some groups but poorer in others.

This long-term research has been directed for decades by two leading British ecologists, George Peterken and Edward Mountford. They found that the changes were not entirely natural as several introduced species had a marked impact. By the 1980s browsing by growing numbers of deer was inhibiting regeneration of trees and other vegetation, such as bramble, in the gaps created by a drought in 1976. There were small numbers of fallow deer here since the Middle Ages but the lack of management in the reserve had led to the local herd using the woodland as a refuge. Bark stripping by the invasive American grey squirrel caused loss of branches and deformation in mature beech trees. While the wood is dominated by native tree species, invasive sycamore seeds blow into the reserve and grow into trees that have to be removed. Finally, forestry operations near the reserve have increased the rate of windthrow – the collapse of mature trees – on the margins of the woodland.

In the words of the main researchers, Peterken and Mountford, the original assumption that a reserve would be 'natural' if it were protected from direct intervention by people, now seems naïve. During the 1990s, as deer browsing and grazing became ever more intense, we have been forced to concede that we are no longer studying natural woodland with moderate herbivore influence, and that increasingly we find ourselves studying a transition to wood pasture.

But is there a place for rewilding in the restoration of Ireland's native woodland? Declan Little, now Lead Ecologist in Coillte Nature, thinks that this concept can be adapted for the Irish situation. His discussion paper, published by Woodlands of Ireland, concludes,

> in the Irish context there are considerable limitations with respect to critical mass and scale, especially due to multiple land ownership and the unavailability of large tracts of land. Nonetheless, rewilding is possible at a modest scale, primarily in the publicly-owned lands, which would have multiple benefits in the presence of other habitats in a landscape matrix.

However, Declan considers that

> ongoing management, especially to control invasive
> species, reduce overgrazing and deliver specific
> ecosystem services, is also a factor that must be
> part of 'minimum intervention management' of
> 'wilderness' in the Irish context to ensure that the
> restoration process achieves maximum biodiversity
> and structural complexity.[101]

Even if woodland managers were able to remove all
impacts of human interference and the invasive species
or grazing animals, it is now clear that climate change is
already having a significant effect on woodland communities of plants and animals. A study by botanists at
Trinity College Dublin, which modelled the responses
of over a hundred characteristic woodland species in
Ireland, found that almost half of them were expected
to lose habitats, with the largest range contraction
projected for the ringlet butterfly. Some species were
predicted to benefit from climate change, with the
brown hairstreak butterfly and alder buckthorn
having the largest potential for expansion from their
current ranges. All species with limited long-range

dispersal possibilities were predicted to lose some of their current range, including a decrease of a half for thin-spiked wood sedge down to 11 per cent contraction for St Patrick's cabbage. These results have significant implications for the future of woodlands in Ireland. Conservation management plans need greater focus on potential climate change impacts in order to ensure the long-term survival of these habitats.[102]

Much as I would like to think that our woodland is in charge of its own destiny, I know that it has been changed by people over the centuries in various ways – by tree-cutting, livestock grazing, introduced species and probably other ways of which I am unaware. Human-induced climate change is already altering the composition of woodland communities making them 'non-natural'. Before the woodland can 'do its own thing' we need to right these wrongs and reset the system to a more natural path.

### Wolves in Ireland?

Rewilding enthusiasts are very keen on the reintroduction to our landscapes of large predators such as wolves, which were exterminated centuries ago. In October 2019 Green Party leader Eamon Ryan called for the reintroduction of the animals to help rewild part of the countrywide. He said that their reintroduction would create a real sense of wilderness and help develop more resilient woodlands. This idea was floated by the English journalist George Monbiot who wrote in his book *Feral* about the dramatic changes that followed the reintroduction of wolves to Yellowstone National Park in the USA.

> A trophic cascade occurs when the animals at the top of the food chain – the large predators – change the numbers not just of their prey, but also of species with which they have no direct connection. Their impacts cascade down through the food chain, in some cases radically changing the ecosystem, the landscape and even the chemical composition of the soil and the atmosphere.[103]

Would a similar reintroduction in Ireland have benefits for the reafforestation of Ireland? The wolf itself is traditionally believed to have survived in woodlands much later in Ireland than in Britain. In Ireland, there is good documentary evidence that the wolf was present up to 1786 and may even have survived into the early

1800s.[104] It is amazing to think that the grandparents of
Ned, a previous owner of our land, may have known
that wolves were still in the local woodlands. Much
further back, archaeological evidence suggests that
the wolf was a widespread mammal in ancient Ireland.
Most of the bones have been found in caves with some
of these being dated by radiocarbon techniques. In the
caves on Keshcorran Hill, County Sligo, a wolf jawbone
was found and dated to around 11,150 years before the
present, about the same time the last Ice Age was finally
ending and vegetation was returning to the landscape.
I walked up to these caves once and found myself
imagining wolf packs using the caves to shelter from
the icy winds that swept across an exposed landscape,
not unlike the tundra of the arctic today where wolves
still survive. They may have hunted such prey as arctic
lemmings and the arctic hare, as they do in northern
Canada today.

The changeover of wolves from this open post-
glacial landscape to one covered by forest, within a
thousand years, shows the adaptability of this species.
When humans first colonised Ireland the small bands of
people would have been in competition with wolf packs
for the same prey. But even in the earliest known human

settlements, such as Mount Sandel, County Derry, there are remains of wolf bones suggesting an early link between the two hunters. Kevin Hickey has suggested that humans and wolves may have shared the same caves for shelter and that there may even have been early domestication, as wolf cubs were captured and reared by humans to assist with tracking and hunting large prey animals. Domestic dogs were quite rare in Europe in this period. However, in later millennia, wolf-dogs were bred from the wild wolf and later the Irish wolfhound was specially bred to help hunt down the wolves themselves. Along with this hunting pressure, the ancient forests were being cleared rapidly and the principal habitat of the wolves was significantly reduced.[105]

The possible reintroduction of wolves to Ireland is probably far away in the future. It is likely that they would have a beneficial effect in reducing the overpopulation of deer and thus helping native woodland to recover. However, a typical wolf pack may need a hunting range of many square kilometres to find enough prey. Such large unoccupied areas are currently absent in Ireland and farmers, especially those with sheep, would be strongly opposed to any attempt to reintroduce this large predator which could affect their livelihoods. The depredations of stray dogs near towns is a constant reminder of the damage that packs of canines can inflict. With our highly modified landscape, wilderness simply does not exist here and there is no real prospect of survival for a wide-ranging predator like the wolf in the foreseeable future.

### Storm damage

The wind has been howling all night with such ferocity that I thought some slates might lift off the roof. Storm Ophelia is the name the meteorologists have given this massive disturbance in the north Atlantic. The radio has been giving weather warnings all through the previous day and predicting widespread disruption. It is the tail end of a tropical hurricane and it is enough to wake me several times in the night.

I rise at first light and head over to the land to see if our polytunnels are still intact. One door has blown open but no other damage is evident so I walk down the meadow and into the wood. Leaves and twigs are everywhere on the ground. It is as if the surplus growth of a thousand trees has been discarded, decluttering the canopy and making way for next year's leaves. As I emerge on the opposite side of the wood it seems brighter than usual and then, I notice it. A giant alder tree has crashed to the ground opening up a great gap in the canopy. Its branches are everywhere, squashing holly trees and blocking the woodland path. I find the place where the tree stood and the reason it has succumbed to the storm. The whole base was rotten in the centre, the heartwood vanished as age overtook it. As the tree crashed the remaining sapwood has ripped apart exposing shredded timber with a deep red colour. I can reach my arm right up the centre of the fallen trunk without touching the top of the cavity.

And then I notice some white fluffy spheres hanging inside the rotten trunk. They look just like cotton wool balls, about the size of a euro coin, suspended by a delicate thread from the wood. With some anticipation I rush home to check my identification guides and my suspicions are confirmed. These are the egg sacks of a cave spider. The adults are nowhere to be seen but, as they normally live their entire lives in darkness, I am sure they have found some other cavity to hide in. The cave spider seeks out places free from light, often in natural caves or old mines though they can sometimes be seen outside as they will emerge around dusk to hunt. Like Spiderman in the movies they can use a single

silk line to swing down and surprise their prey. They
are often found in dark cavities that are used by bats
although the connections between the two species are
poorly known. In this woodland there are no caves so
hollow trees are the best alternative we can offer this
specialised inhabitant.

Deadwood habitats directly support a great many
specialist plants and animals – known as 'saproxylic'
organisms. Overall, it has been estimated that 13 per
cent of all species of plants and animals known in
the UK are directly dependent on deadwood habitats,
while many more are dependent upon the saproxylic
organisms themselves. In woodland habitats dead or
decaying wood may be essential for up to a third of
all the species that call it home. It provides a habitat
for many species of bryophytes (mosses and liverworts),
lichens, fungi, invertebrates, fish, amphibians, reptiles,
birds and mammals. Studies on overturned tree stumps,
caused by windblow, also show interesting changes in
soil disruption and biodiversity over time.

Despite this essential role, deadwood has been
removed from woodland ecosystems for thousands
of years, usually as fuel but often just to 'tidy up'.
Deadwood is often viewed simplistically as standing

snags or fallen dead tree material and logs. In fact, there is a huge range of deadwood micro-habitats that may be found within these categories, as well as on living trees – in particular, living veteran trees provide many important deadwood habitats. Dry rot holes, wet rot holes, rotting heartwood and decaying sap under bark are all examples of deadwood micro-habitats. In addition to these terrestrial habitats, deadwood that is fully or partially submerged in water provides essential micro-habitats for a variety of fish and freshwater invertebrates. The majority of saproxylic creatures are not specific to particular types of trees but do need specialised micro-habitats. Many of these are threatened through loss of habitat. As well as being key links in the woodland ecosystem through nutrient cycling, soil creation and food for other animals, saproxylic invertebrates create new habitats within deadwood, and their bodies themselves also provide habitats for other animals, such as parasitoid wasps which lay their eggs within the larvae of wood wasps and longhorn beetles that live within fallen deadwood.

I am getting curious now, so I lift a few dead logs that have been lying on the woodland floor for years. Most have scurrying isopods – as children we called them slaters. There are also slugs and snails, centipedes and beetles, tiny mites and spiders. In fact, a whole community is living off the decaying cellulose in the tree. There are holes bored in the wood and some of them are occupied by small white grubs. Out of one dead branch runs a beautiful animal called the black-spotted longhorn beetle. I replace the logs in their original positions to try to restore the habitats that these creatures need.

*The National Survey of Native Woodlands* found that fine and coarse woody debris were the most abundant types of deadwood in Irish broadleaf woods. Standing dead or damaged trees were much less common and uprooted and snapped trees were largely rare or absent.[106] Our woodland has plenty of damaged standing trunks and broken branches and these are exploited by birds that nest in cavities, such as the tits and starlings, while the woodpeckers have drilled nest holes in at least four decaying trees.

Decay in wood is often betrayed by the appearance of fungi on the surface. Some fungi such as the fly agaric are called 'mycorrhizas', meaning 'fungus root'. Most dramatic are the huge bracket fungi that usually grow on the trunks of living trees. However, the underground networks of fungi are the most amazing features of these organisms. Fungi live around trees and other plant roots and help them to grow by capturing water and nutrients in their vast networks of filaments called mycelia and supplying these to the tree. In return, the trees give the fungi sugars from photosynthesis.

Emerging ideas suggest that the fungal mycelia are like a vast network of pipes and cables beneath the soil, transferring information, water and chemicals around the forest ecosystem. The hypotheses in Peter Wohlleben's book *The Hidden Life of Trees* suggest forest ecosystems should be thought of as integrated communities rather than stands of individual trees.[107] If true, this altruistic behaviour – trees helping out a neighbour in trouble – could support some weaker individuals to survive drought by sharing resources. The multiple roles of fungi in decomposition, nutrient recycling and communication between plants in a woodland are all poorly understood but clearly vital for the healthy functioning of the ecosystem.

### Fungal forays

I notice a greater range of fungi in the woodland this autumn – some on the ground, others on the trunks of living trees and still more growing on dead twigs and branches. So, I contact Paul Dowding, a lecturer in botany while I was at university who has now retired to manage his own native woodland. Paul is an expert on fungi and joint author of a fascinating guide called *Forest Fungi in Ireland* that not only identifies the species but provides recipes for adding them to meals. Together we explore our wood, searching in the leaf litter and on dead branches and in a few hours, we make a list of thirty-four species of fungi. Some are familiar such as the fly agaric, the classic red and white toadstool often pictured with a leprechaun sitting on it. I haven't seen any little people in our wood yet but I have found several fly agarics growing on the roots of birch trees. Other fungi that we find are new to me and have fascinating common names such as amethyst deceiver, wood woolly foot and blushing bracket. The fungi are good indicators that the wood is long established and little disturbed.

Peter Wyse Jackson assures us in his book *Ireland's Generous Nature* that wild-collected fungi do not seem to have been widely gathered and used in historical times.[108] There is little reference to them in the standard culinary or herbalist books of previous centuries. People were generally afraid of consuming mushrooms due to stories about poisoning incidents and a lack of general knowledge about their identification. Perhaps the association of fungi with the death and decay of trees was another reason why they were avoided. Paul Dowding says that in Ireland all fungi, apart from the field mushroom, were known as 'pookies' and were absolutely avoided. This contrasts with other countries such as China and Japan where mushrooms were cultivated and eaten for thousands of years. In Europe by the 1800s eating mushrooms was popular and some countries had enacted laws to prevent the sale of dangerous fungi.[109]

We know relatively little about the potential diversity of fungal species in native woodlands, largely because the ancient woods were so depleted by the early nineteenth century when much natural history recording began. The few unmanaged old woods that have persisted through the centuries have veteran trees that contain the widest range of fungi. A key is the presence of standing dead trees and decaying wood left to rot on the ground. Lack of disturbance to the soil and leaf litter also helps to preserve the essential fungal mycelia that support the fruiting bodies we see above ground. Our woodland has many of these characteristics which should make it a valuable habitat for less common fungi. I look forward to collecting some of the fruiting bodies where I can be sure of their identification and cooking them for breakfast in the wood with the help of Paul's book.

## Oak returns

I am amazed at the rapid response of the ground vegetation in the clearings that we have created by removing sycamores and thinning holly trees in the canopy. In the first growing season the bare ground becomes a paradise of ferns – the broad buckler, hard fern and lady fern being the most abundant. Their spreading fronds give the woodland floor a tropical appearance before they start to be overtaken by brambles. In between the ferns are small tree seedlings, including sycamore, of course. But there are also ash, birch, alder and holly seedlings with their distinctive leaf shapes. And then oak seedlings start to appear late into the summer when others are already well established. The acorns must have lain here in the woodland soil, before the warming sunlight stimulated them to germinate. I start to find tiny oaks all over the clearings. To prevent them being browsed by deer, I use some left-over plastic rabbit guards to cover them when they are small and vulnerable.

There are only three mature pedunculate oaks in the wood so the acorns are most likely to have come from them. They get their name from the peduncle or stalk that holds the acorn to the twig until it ripens and either falls to the ground or is carried off by a bird or a squirrel. Inevitably some of these seeds are dropped or never eaten and may be lucky to end up in a place with just the right conditions to germinate. It is exciting to find that nature is doing the job of natural regeneration, so I don't have to rely completely on tree planting to fill the gaps in the woodland.

While oak is currently a scarce tree in our woodland, it may not have been so in the past. Oak seedlings do not grow well in shady conditions and when old trees fall, their place in the canopy is often taken by faster-growing species such as birch, alder or ash. I would love to get some more oak back into the woodland as it is an amazing species, rich in biodiversity and useful for many purposes. Although we have only two native oak species in Ireland there are over five hundred members of the *Quercus* genus worldwide. Found in all continents (except Antarctica) oaks come in all shapes and sizes – deciduous and evergreen, from dwarf shrubs to giant spreading forest trees – with enormous diversity in leaf

shape, bark patterns and acorn designs.[110] Throughout
the temperate regions of the world oak has sustained
many human societies by providing food, fuel, building
materials, bark for tanning leather, wooden ships and
casks to store the food and drink that provisioned
western civilisations in past centuries.

There is no more common tree in heraldry than the
oak which is associated with strength, stability and
good character. The people of Britain were said to have
'hearts of oak' and this is most celebrated by their resistance to Nazi invasion at the start of the Second World
War. To the ancient Greeks, oak was connected with the
god Zeus. To the Vikings it was their god Thor's tree.
Isaiah, predicting the redemption of Israel in the Bible
wrote 'they will be called oaks of righteousness, the
planting of the Lord, to display his glory' (Isaiah 61:3).[111]

An American natural history writer, Linda Mapes,
lived intimately for a full year with a single hundred-
year-old oak tree in Harvard Forest in the USA. With
the help of a range of academic researchers she explored
every aspect of the tree from its leaves to the roots and
associated network of mycelia underground. She had
a hammock suspended in the canopy from where she
was able to observe the minutiae of life in her 'witness

tree' – 'hairy couplets of gypsy moth caterpillars, spiders climbing way faster than me'.[112]

Of all our native trees, oaks harbour the most diverse community of animals and plants living on their leaves, flowers, acorns, bark, roots and in the decaying wood. In the UK a comprehensive inventory found that a total of at least 2,300 species were known to use oak trees as a habitat. Those species found only on oak and never on other trees included 257 invertebrates (insects and other small creatures), fifty-seven fungi and twelve lichens.[113] Not only have oaks played a key role in our history, but they themselves also provide important micro-habitats for a unique community of other plants and animals.

### Saving seeds

When I decided to plant some of our farmland with native trees, I discovered that there was a shortage of young native oaks from the nurseries. This is under-standable as the native oak trees in Ireland only produce a good acorn crop once every two to six years for pedunculate oak and every three to eight years for sessile oak.[114] The trees must reach the grand old age of forty to fifty years old before they produce their first good seed crop. To add to the shortage of acorns, many woodland oaks are too crowded by their neighbours so the lack of sunlight prevents good flowering or seed production in most years.

The obvious answer is to collect my own acorns and plant them out. But where do I get the seed? To learn more, I joined a course in seed collection that was hosted by Woodlands of Ireland and the government Forest Service. On a beautiful September morning, a mixed group of enthusiasts gathered in a church hall in Killeshandra, County Cavan, to learn the techniques from experienced seed collectors and nurserymen. In the afternoon we followed the seed collectors and watched them identify the best trees and collect seed by shaking the branches with long hooks to knock them to the ground. After the course finished, I registered with the Forest Service as a collector of native tree seed.

Fortunately, there is a line of enormous pedunculate oaks along the road that leads to our woodland. I suspect that they were planted more than two hundred years ago by Francis Synge, the enterprising landlord in this part of Wicklow, who established several hundred thousand trees on his estate. Even more fortunately, the autumn that I decide to venture into the nursery business is a good year for acorns. The road surface and the grass in the neighbouring field are littered with the beautiful seeds in their round cups. Of course, all the local crows are delighted. Rooks, magpies, hoodies and jays gather in flocks to feast on the bounty. Jays are often accredited with burying large numbers of acorns, some of which they never return to, thus inadvertently planting new oak trees. Squirrels also bury acorns to store for the winter and may forget where they are secreted away. At night, I suspect that the badgers from the nearby sett come over to forage beneath the giant oak trees as the acorns help them to fatten up for the winter ahead. Every day in October I return to find a new crop on the ground and the bags of acorns begin to accumulate. I wonder what other trees I can grow from seed.

The fallen alder tree in the woodland provides a rare opportunity to collect some of the tiny cones that grow in the canopy, now lying on the ground. I fill a few bags with the small brown fruits and take them home to dry and extract the seed. The seeds are smaller than sugar grains and black as pepper. A good shake of the bag is enough to remove them from the cones. Planting out is a bit more complicated. I am storing them in paper envelopes for the winter and will plant out in the spring. They need to be stratified a month before sowing. This means storing them in a fridge to simulate the frosty conditions that help to kick-start germination. I broadcast the seed thinly onto a damp seed compost in a series of trays and then leave them outdoors to get the sunlight and rain. Unfortunately, I put them in an out-of-the-way place and forgot to water the trays so some will not survive to the spring. Perhaps it's time to get some professional advice on this.

One of the best guides to growing Ireland's native trees was published as *Our Trees* in the year 2000 as part of the People's Millennium Forests Project. The collection, storage, treatment and sowing of tree seed is a skill that needs to be learned just like gardening. This year I am also trying to propagate the seeds of rowan (mountain ash) and hazel. It looks like a good year with large crops of each. Seed collection, especially for the berried trees, has to be timed so that the fruit is ripe but not yet eaten by birds. I have made a trip to Glendasan in the Wicklow Mountains National Park where rowan trees grow abundantly by the waterfall. Here they are sure to be from native stock and can survive on the poorest soils and in quite harsh conditions. I collect the berries in bags when they are beginning to turn scarlet. The red pigment in the berries contains a germination inhibitor which brings on dormancy and reduces the number of seeds that will develop in spring. I bring the bags of ripe berries home and macerate them, washing the pulp away and extracting the small, hard seeds. These are then stratified in horticultural sand in seed trays and left for planting in the spring.

Nut-bearing trees are much easier to propagate for planting. The hazel trees have a great crop this autumn too. The beautiful green nuts form in clusters of up to four or five, like flower arrangements at the tips of branches. One problem for the seed collector is that, if picked too early, they are often either undeveloped or rotten, so I test a sample of the nuts each day. If I miss the right time to harvest, many nuts will have already dropped to the ground where they provide a bonanza for mice and squirrels. The little circular hole at one end surrounded by characteristic tooth marks is typical of a hazelnut opened by a wood mouse. The squirrels split the shells down the middle and hide away the bulk of the nuts in their winter larder. The jays are feasting now on the nuts and make a lot of noise in the wood as they do so.

Picking the nuts from the trees is less desirable as they are often soft and tasteless and may quickly wither in the shells. When they are ripe, they will readily drop from the husks and a gentle shake of the branches usually produces a rain of nuts. They can be stored in a dry tin to keep the mice at bay or planted out immediately in some damp soil to sleep for the winter. I am delighted to see that we have a good crop of naturally regenerating hazels in the clearings where the old hazel trees were coppiced last winter. Hazelnuts have been a valuable food item for people in Ireland from earliest times. Archaeological excavations from as early as 8,000 years ago have produced the hard shells of these nuts and they were also found in the Viking settlements in Dublin. This indicates how widespread hazelwoods were in the Irish landscape in ancient times. Early laws in Old Irish even mention that a hungry person was entitled to gather a handful of hazelnuts from a privately owned wood.[115] I hope that any ravaging hordes of the future will overlook our lovely woodland!

Reading the manuals, I discover that it is best to plant hazelnuts and acorns in soil as soon as possible and not to let them dry out. I have bought a batch of extra deep seed trays each with dozens of small compartments and, with the help of family and friends, I set about the task of planting by pushing each seed just under the surface of some compost in rows and rows of trays. When the job is finished, I am amazed that we have planted a total of over two thousand individual acorns and hundreds of other tree seeds. I have constructed a table made of old pallets outdoors where they will be off the ground to make it more difficult for mice to dig them up and I cover the trays with a fine mesh fabric that will discourage raids by crows yet let the rain reach them. I can't believe that these will all germinate but I must be patient and let nature take its course. As the winter slowly passes, I check them regularly and, when the rain is scarce, I sprinkle the trays with water to keep the seeds moist. I know that, just below the surface, a miracle is happening. Each acorn or hazelnut has split its outer husk and pushed out a long white root that reaches downward in the soil searching for water and nutrients. The nut itself is like a packed lunch that the adult tree has sent with each one of its offspring to help it on its way.

By April the first shoots of the oaks are beginning to push up from the soil. At first these are blood red in colour – just tiny stumps emerging into the light.

Then the first leaves appear, small and delicate green colour, to gather sunlight. It is time to remove the fabric and let them soak up the sunshine. Now the leaves are manufacturing sugars through the wondrous process of photosynthesis. They are like tiny solar panels gathering the rays of sunshine and turning them into energy for the new plant. Each day there are more mini oak trees and the trays are beginning to fill with green. Hazels, rowans and alders are starting to appear too and I must care for them in these vulnerable early months. Incredibly, most of the seeds appear to have germinated and now I have an abundance of new life that will need to find a forest home. After a year in the seed trays, the thousands of tiny trees will be planted out in specially prepared ground about the size of a tennis court. Here they will grow on for a year or two until they are up to half a metre in height and ready to be transplanted into their final homes in the new native woodland plantation.

### Forest schools

Today I am out with my granddaughter, Ivy, searching for the last of the blackberries which we both love to eat. Last week we started to build a treehouse together in the wood. It reminded me so much of my own childhood as we hauled planks up into the lower branches of a giant ash. Our grandchildren are one of the reasons I bought our woodland. I want them to enjoy the unrestrained pleasure of outdoor play and learn the practical skills that will serve them in later life as resources become scarce in the world.

I learned many of these skills by trial and error in the fields and woods around my childhood home and later at scout camps in the woodlands of Powerscourt Estate in Wicklow. I still have on my shelves a dog-eared copy of *Scouting for Boys: A Handbook for Instruction in Good Citizenship,* which shows how to make a bivouac from sticks and leaves. Children in richer countries today are largely out of touch with nature. A recent survey of 2,000 families with children below the age of fourteen found that, on average, they were spending over three hours a day on electronic devices – much more than they spent outdoors. They can tell you a lot about the catastrophic loss of the Amazon rainforests, about the climate crisis and the extinction of species, but not about the last time they explored a woodland or waded in a stream. Often, they know little about nature on their own doorsteps and they have not learned the basic skills of building a shelter, lighting a fire or finding their food in wilder surroundings. Richard Louv coined the term 'nature-deficit disorder' to describe this modern disconnect between children and the natural environment. He wrote, 'at the moment that the bond is breaking between the young and the natural world, a growing body of research links our mental, physical and spiritual health directly to our association with nature – in positive ways'.[116]

In recent years, there are some people who have tried to address this deficit by allowing children to experience life in the woods. Forest schools have been developed all over the country providing children of all ages with opportunities to visit the same local woodlands on a regular basis to learn through play about the natural environment, how to handle risks and, most impor-tantly, to use their own initiative to solve problems and cooperate with others. Of course, safety in the wild is paramount but within a safe, supervised environment there is room for great imaginary play, experimentation and learning of practical skills. I don't think I would have learnt how to light a fire from foraged wood and kindling unless I had tried and failed many times myself.

To find out what actually happens in a forest school, I join some children and their leaders in an outdoor class at the old estate of Altidore in County Wicklow. From the eighteenth century on this estate was in the ownership of the Emmet family, which included the United Irishman Thomas Addis Emmet and the patriot Robert Emmet. The present owner, Philip Emmet, now runs Altidore Farm where he produces certified organic beef and lamb for sale in a local butcher's shop. The estate also has fine woodlands of oak and many other broadleaved trees. Some of these trees are centuries old and could be described as veterans.

There is a fine drizzle falling as we gather among the trees but this doesn't seem to bother the children who are brimming over with excitement. First, the leaders play some wide games with them to burn off the excess energy. Then they sit in a large circle on cut logs to sing songs about the woodland. After a few minutes they set off in different directions to collect some acorns from the ground beneath the giant oaks while I put out a line of empty milk cartons for the children to fill one each with dark woodland soil. In their carton they plant an acorn, firm it down and water it well to keep it alive. Each child will take one home and care for it over the winter, returning in the spring to plant a new tree in the woodland clearing. The older children divide up into teams and play a game that teaches them to read tracks and signs in the woodland and make sure that they can move about and leave no trace. Each has adopted the name of a woodland animal – badger, buzzard, pine marten, woodpecker. Without realising it they are becoming accustomed to close encounters with the natural world, overcoming any fears that they may have had about the wild and working in teams to help each other. With luck some of this will build resilience in the young people and help them as adults to care for woodlands and the rest of nature.

## Close-to-nature forestry

One of the problems that native hardwood forestry has always faced in Ireland is the disconnect between timber production and the market for wood in this country. The monotonous plantations that replaced much of our remaining native woodland during the last couple of centuries were stocked with conifers sourced from the Pacific region of North America. There these same species *are* native and we can learn much from the experience of American foresters how to manage a native forest resource. While the climate in the north-west coastal states of the USA is similar to

that in Ireland, the flora and fauna are totally different
– separated by an ocean and a continent for millions of
years.

An October holiday in this remote area provided me
with an opportunity to see these trees in their natural
surroundings. Deep in the coastal range of mountains
in the state of Oregon there is a unique group of forests
that are being managed by one family in a way that
harks back to the Native Americans who have called
this place home for millennia. The spokesman for the
family is Peter Hayes, an educationalist, naturalist and
forest manager who sees the forests not just as a source
of timber for profit but as a multifunctional resource
that can benefit a whole community.

I joined a group of forestry specialists on a walk
around one of these forests at a time when maples
and oaks lit up the woodland with beautiful yellow
and red colours of the fall. The dominant native tree
here is the Douglas fir but these forest giants are quite
different from the blanket monocultural conifer plantations that we see in Britain and Ireland. For a start, the
trees are massive – up to 30 metres in height – and with
basal stems as wide as a door. The autumn sunlight
pouring through the forest canopy produces a diverse

undergrowth with abundant regeneration of young native trees such as red alder, vine maple and Pacific yew. I felt dwarfed by this mighty forest in comparison to the compact nature of my own woodland at home. I had to keep pinching myself as a reminder that although this appeared like an undisturbed, old-growth forest, it was essentially a commercial plantation.

Hayes explains that their approach is similar to continuous cover forestry in Europe where the thinning focuses on removing the weaker individual trees to give space and light for the better-quality specimens to prosper and grow. They also replant in the spaces to increase the diversity of the forest so that it will be more resilient to climate change and pathogens such as laminated root rot which has already hit the fir trees. In fact, this enterprise only removes about 20 per cent of the annual growth in the forest leaving the majority of timber volume in the standing trees.

Because the local sawmills are not set up for processing all of the varied types and sizes of timber that Hyla Woods produces, the Hayes family has established its own small milling operation with a solar-powered drying kiln to finish the high-quality product. They work with small-scale customers who are prepared to pay a premium for sustainably harvested timber from an ecologically healthy forest. I paid a visit to one of these customers, The Joinery, in nearby Portland. Here I met Martina Kaiwi who showed me the fine craftmanship that turns Hyla timber into finished products like unique polished tables and chairs as well as intricate wooden toys and decorative pieces.

Peter Hayes is just one of a long family line of foresters that goes back to his great-great-grandfather who logged timber in the forests of the eastern states. He shows me old photographs of the loggers working with hand saws and axes to fell mature trees and the steam-driven winches that hauled the logs to the edge of the forest. Selling up and moving west, as the forests of the Pacific states were opened up, the family bought holdings that had been neglected over the years. Before Europeans arrived in the 1700s, the original old-growth forest of the Pacific Rim stretched virtually unbroken for nearly two thousand miles from Alaska almost to San Francisco. When white settlers first came to Oregon they found a beautiful land of open forests with massive trees but, following a century of exploiting and mismanaging these forests, they were left with a hugely depleted landscape.[117] The Hayes family introduced a type of forestry that aimed to improve the habitats, involve the local communities and provide an income for its members. Several generations later, Hayes explains that his son, Ben, and daughter, Molly, have now taken up the baton in this long-running relay.

Hayes has emerged as a local spokesman for creating forestry markets that recognise what he calls 'high conservation-value forestry'. These markets reward forest owners for 'ecosystem services' like preserving wildlife habitats, storing carbon and keeping waterways cool and clean. And they're essential to allow small woodland owners like him to grow forests that are both ecologically complex and economically viable. As we walked down the steep slopes, deeply marked with the tracks of elk, I could hear the sound of a creek running between the trees. The water flows through a series of logpiles, some of which have been placed here to improve aquatic habitats, and other forest debris that has been washed down by frequent floods. In December, the migratory Coho salmon arrive back to spawn in the gravels and pools of these headwater creeks and the Hayes family organises a local celebration here to welcome their return, just as the indigenous tribes did centuries before. And beavers have returned too, creating more natural dams and restoring the river to a sinuous channel.

Although this seems like a completely natural environment, Hayes explains that it is actively managed and that this intervention is the key to a healthy habitat. 'We run a profitable forestry business here,' he says, 'but we define profit in a uniquely broad way. Our highest priority is to improve the health of the forest. Our feeling is that, if we make a profit at the expense of the land then it is basically a form of theft.' Their operation uses barely any herbicides, they thin groves out to allow more sunlight in with no clear-felling and, instead of a monoculture, they plant up to a dozen tree species to diversify the forest. 'What we want', says Hayes, 'is a forest with multiple species and trees of multiple ages. This an experimental project and our dream is to have a working model that shows how you can have a forest that is economically viable but not at the expense of losing the health and wealth of the land.' I could not help comparing this approach to the neglect of old woods in some private Irish estates or to the common practice of forestry in Ireland based on single-species monocultures grown for clear-felling and quick return.

A key to this experiment is recording accurately many aspects of the forests' function. There are regular stock assessments of the volume of standing timber in each plot of the 1,000 acres of forest. Plant and bird species are carefully monitored and Hayes can reel off many tree species that have found their own way back to these forests. A committed educationalist, he hands me a list of research projects that have been undertaken by academics in these forests with results that feed straight back into his management methods. He estimates too that the carbon being captured in these forests is increasing annually and is currently about fifty times the amount of carbon produced by his family business in a typical year. This is an outstanding example of sustainable forestry that is combining a healthy forest ecosystem and a viable business model with developing local markets for high-quality timber products. It can teach us much about how to manage Ireland's native woodland into the future.

## *Future forests – Long life*

William Byrne took over the farm from his father
Ned at a time of great political upheaval in Ireland.
Members of the Irish Volunteers were training in the
local forests with weapons smuggled from Germany.
The local children would go to the woods the following
day and collect the spent cartridges lying around
among the trees. After the 1916 Rising in Dublin, a
guerrilla war, led by Michael Collins, targeted British
troops and policemen. The Black and Tans carried
out regular searches for rebels in the local area. Once,
when the soldiers were coming up the road beneath
the line of oak trees, children from the houses ran into
the neighbouring fields and hid beneath a haystack.
This was a dangerous move as the Black and Tans

often set fire to all the hay on a farm in the search
for insurgents.

The oak trees along the road were over a century old
in the 1920s when the Anglo-Irish Treaty was signed and
the Irish Free State came into being. But this had little
immediate benefit for the local people of our area. Rural
poverty, which had been a feature of the area since the
Famine, became worse as the fledgling state struggled
without British support. Dublin was a city of packed
tenements, abject poverty for the bulk of the inhabitants
and there was no help for people without work. Most
of Ned's surviving family had emigrated to America in
search of a better life. William, now in his fifties, was
finding it difficult to manage the farm on his own and
was losing money. He was unmarried and lonely so he
moved in with a relative in the local village. Eventually,
he decided to emigrate to join his younger brother in
America. A year later the farm and woodland were sold
at auction and the long involvement of Ned's family with
this land came to an end.

When I stand in the woodland, I can imagine Ned
and his family working to save firewood for the winter
over a century before. His youngest son, Dan, worked
as a woodsman for the local estate and he brought home

the skills of coppicing, the traces of which I can still see in the older trees today. Cutting certain trees to the ground and allowing them to regenerate over a cycle of years effectively prolongs the life of these plants indefinitely. Properly managed, a coppiced wood can last for many hundreds of years, sustaining generations of workers and a rich wildlife. Unmanaged, most trees have a natural lifespan passing through youth, maturity and old age just like ourselves.

Trees are the longest-living individual organisms in the world. Think of the Californian redwood trees that could be up to 2,200 years old. In Europe, there is a yew tree living in the churchyard of Llangernyw village in North Wales which is estimated to be at least 4,000 years old. It is believed to have taken root sometime during the Bronze Age. Experts can't agree which tree is the oldest in Ireland. Wexford-based archaeologist Colm Moriarty thinks it might be the Silken Thomas yew in Maynooth, which is about 800 years old. Legend has it that Silken Thomas played a lute under the boughs of the tree the night before he surrendered to King Henry VIII in the 1500s. Colin Kelleher is a botanist in the National Botanic Gardens. He worked on the genetics of Irish oaks so I asked him whether he thought these

long-lived trees could rival the yew's longevity. He says
that several oak trees are so old they also have names.
The Brian Bóru oak in County Clare is 'one of the top
five, if not top three' oldest trees in Ireland. It reportedly
dates from the time of Brian Bóru, who was born nearby
in 941AD. It is difficult to date trees accurately without
cores being taken and, for such an old tree, that would
be too much of a risk. Few trees in Ireland would be
older than this although some native woods have stood
throughout the rise and fall of the human population.
Yet we have failed to protect most of them over the last
century.

## Perceptions of the wildwoods

In ancient times trees and woodlands were revered as
sacred. Some even considered that they represented
the spirits of lost ancestors who were watching over
the present people. Trees feature in the earliest written
records of cultural Ireland where, from at least the
fourth to the ninth century AD, Ogham, an alphabet
of twenty letters, can be found on over 300 stone
monuments around the country. Known as the 'Celtic
Tree Alphabet', each of its characters, or 'trees', is made
out of a vertical reference line, or 'stem', with one or

more slashes, or 'twigs', which make up the letters of the Irish language. The words are read vertically from bottom to top. The sacred sites of pre-Christian Ireland were *nemeton* or groves of trees and individual revered trees were called *bile*. Inaugural ceremonies for tribal chieftains were performed under such trees.[118]

As the remaining native woodlands were rapidly exploited, the woodland creatures retreated into smaller and smaller refuges. At the same time, the attitudes of Ireland's people to the woodlands changed. In ancient times, the extensive forests were a source of game, fruits and shelter but also represented a dangerous place where people could be ambushed by hostile tribes or predatory animals. Wolves were so numerous in the woods of early medieval Ireland as to constitute a formidable danger to the community.[119] Extensive woodlands also gave refuge to other wild animals – the fox, pine marten and predatory birds – all of which occasionally hunted livestock. By removing their cover, it was possible to reduce populations of these species and their depredations on farming. Up to the nineteenth century, woodland was regarded mainly in utilitarian terms. It provided an apparently endless source of material for building, fuel, farm implements, fencing, boats, wooden barrels, charcoal-making and many other uses. It seemed as if there were no limits to its exploitation.

Colonising forces, and the estate owners that followed, saw the few remaining natural forests as an extension of their property and as a ready source of the large timbers needed to build the thousands of ships required by the Royal Navy to rule the dominions of the British Empire. The population expansion that preceded the Great Famines of the mid-nineteenth century led to scouring of the remaining timber for fuel and many other uses. The small fragments of original woodland that remained were generally within the walls of the great estates, often owned by absentee landlords. It is unlikely that the native woodlands, that now fill the Killarney valley in County Kerry, would have survived had they not been part of the Bourne-Vincent estate (now within Killarney National Park). In these great estates there was also management of the woods by coppicing to produce a continuing supply of timber. This was encouraged by some of the landed gentry and extensive planting was also undertaken in the Wicklow estates such as Powerscourt and Coolatin. Tree planting was supported by the (later Royal) Dublin Society by means of grants and incentives. Trees were was also essential for healthy populations of deer and pheasants that were prized game for the sport of a privileged few.

Now the need for protection and husbandry was beginning to replace pure exploitation of the woods. The end of the nineteenth century also saw the start of forestry practices as we know them today. Trials were undertaken with exotic trees from all around the world but especially with the conifers that were brought back from the Pacific coasts of North America. Unfortunately, some invasive species, most notably rhododendron and laurel, were introduced to large estates as cover for game and these inevitably escaped into the remaining native woodlands.

The War of Independence and the emergence of the new Republic of Ireland broke down the walls of the great estates but did not halt the loss of native woodland. Instead, there was a drive to 'reforest' the country for economic purposes but now the target was fast-growing conifer plantations that would help to make the new state less dependent on imported timber. A revisionist history developed, claiming that the British rulers of Ireland had been responsible for the wholesale exploitation of the original forests of Ireland that had covered the country in the centuries before independence. In fact, most of the wildwood had been cleared thousands of years earlier by generations of Irish as a direct effect of the need for more farmland to feed the growing population. The first school of forestry was established at the Avondale estate in County Wicklow where the early planting trials of Samuel Hayes, a previous owner, were continued and extended. At about the same time, Ned's family stopped managing the native woodland that we now own and it was left to its own devices.

By 1970, when the state Forest and Wildlife Service was formed within the Department of Lands, recreational use of forests was becoming a valued pursuit, especially for an increasingly urban population that had largely lost its direct contact with the land. The Open Forest policy for public lands was continued by newly formed forestry company, Coillte Teo, which took over the existing state-owned properties in 1988 although a few fragments of semi-natural woodland were transferred to the Wildlife Service as nature reserves. Unfortunately, the modern Irish state has not given the priority needed to restoring the native woodlands that characterised the early Irish landscape and many are now in very poor condition.

## Why do we need the woods?

I know that my own life would be impoverished if our woodland was destroyed. I would greatly miss the relaxation that a walk in the wood brings and I could never forgive the loss of the badgers, woodpeckers and the rich diversity of species for which this habitat is home. On a practical level, I would no longer have a renewable supply of fuel. Timber, charcoal and many other woodland resources have sustained Irish people over millennia and these habitats continue to provide benefits to our civilisation that we scarcely appreciate. The most important one is that trees absorb carbon dioxide from the air and give out the oxygen that we need to breath. Known in today's terminology as 'ecosystem services', such benefits are free and therefore widely ignored and undervalued.

We know that native woodlands along the banks of rivers and lakes can intercept harmful agricultural runoff preventing it from entering the water and killing fish and other aquatic life. The dappled light that broad-leaved trees cast onto the water surface provides ideal conditions for fish to lie in river pools. Woodlands can regulate the flow of water in rivers, reduce flooding by slowing down the flow off the hills and stabilise banks preventing the damage caused by silt entering the water.

The mental health benefits of a relaxing walk in the woods are just starting to be appreciated in the west while the Japanese have practised the art of *shinrin-yoku*, or forest bathing, for generations. Woodlands are used by forest schools to teach children basic survival skills through play to balance the time that they now spend indoors on electronic devices. They have a key role in combating the modern problem of 'nature-deficit disorder'.

Woodland is the natural vegetation cover on this island. Its three-dimensional structure supports more native species than any other type of habitat including some species that are found nowhere else in Ireland. From woodland fungi to woodpeckers, there are hundreds of specialists that rely on the cover and stability provided by old native trees. About one-fifth of our plant life, over a quarter of breeding birds and half of the native invertebrates are woodland species. If we allow the native woodlands to disappear, we will cause a major extinction of species in Ireland.

### Capturing carbon

I love to stand on a bright morning in one of the clearings that we have created and simply watch the sun's rays shine through the new leaves creating dappled pools of light on the woodland floor. Trees, like other green plants, depend on sunlight to manufacture sugars and other nutrients. They absorb carbon dioxide ($CO_2$), storing carbon above and below ground, and producing oxygen as a by-product of photosynthesis. In the presence of increased greenhouse gases in the atmosphere, forests become even more vital by removing carbon from the atmosphere to mitigate the effects of climate change on the environment. Forests therefore play a specific and important role in the global carbon cycle by absorbing and storing carbon.

The Environmental Protection Agency estimated that total national greenhouse gas emissions in Ireland were the equivalent of over sixty million tonnes of $CO_2$ in 2018. If we could plant enough trees, we could make a significant contribution to capturing some of these gases. Forests in the United States absorb and store about 750 million metric tonnes of $CO_2$ each year, an amount equivalent to ten per cent of the country's emissions. Australian researchers have done some work to estimate the area of land needed to do the job. Based on their calculations, for above- and below-ground biomass of carbon stored per hectare, cool temperate moist forests (such as those in Ireland) store the most carbon at 625 tonnes per hectare. Remember these are averages and in some cases specific forests may be much higher. The researchers found that combining any forest type with predominantly peat soils resulted in a natural carbon storage machine *par excellence*.[120] Ireland's forests are currently in the cool temperate moist category although global warming may change this rather too soon.

Irish Wildlife Trust campaigns officer Pádraic Fogarty says:

> It's now blindingly obvious that we need a programme to bring trees back to our landscapes on a vast scale. However, we need to be strategic about how this is done. Planting monoculture plantations of conifers is not the solution and will only add to problems.

A combination of approaches is needed, based on native trees and ecological processes, to grow more trees in towns, cities and on farms. Fogarty believes

we can create large, permanent forests on public
land, on uplands and along river corridors. We
can have a commercial timber sector based on
close-to-nature techniques and 'continuous cover'.
We should give communities more say in the development of these woodlands to foster ownership
and stewardship.

Natural solutions like widespread tree planting can
help address the climate emergency in three ways –
by reducing greenhouse gas emissions such as carbon
dioxide and methane through converting land from
short-term agriculture to native woodland; by capturing
and storing additional $CO_2$ from the atmosphere; and
by improving the resilience of ecosystems, thereby
helping communities adapt to the increases in storms,
flooding and droughts associated with climate change.
There was a long summer drought in Ireland in 2018,
just after we had planted nearly 7,000 new trees on our
land. The grass in the meadows was brown by July and
the new trees came under serious stress. Some dropped
their leaves early and did not survive till the autumn.
But in the mature native woodland there was shade
and a cooler atmosphere which was a relief from the

blazing sun. The old trees drew water up through their deep root systems and continued to absorb $CO_2$ and release oxygen.

In 2003, Central Europe experienced a severe drought. A team of researchers in Switzerland studied plant–water relations and the response of trees to increased $CO_2$ using experimental methods in a 100-year-old mixed deciduous forest on a slope near Basel. The drought lasted from early June to mid-September and average rates of maximum photosynthesis across all species decreased considerably in mid-August. Of five deciduous tree species studied, daily peak values of sap flow remained surprisingly constant over the whole period in sessile oak and decreased to only about half of typical early summer levels in beech and hornbeam. Although leaves remained longer on these trees in 2003 compared with normal, the growth rate of the stems reached only about 75 per cent of that in previous years. This suggests that the tree species studied, particularly sessile oak, did not experience severe water stress. However, the researchers acknowledged that an increased frequency of such exceptionally dry summers could have a more serious impact than a single event but would give sessile oak a competitive advantage in the long run.[121]

## Redesigning the landscape

The Irish national parliament, the Dáil, among many across the world, has acknowledged that we are already in a climate and biodiversity emergency. So, what is being done to capture some of the carbon that we have been discharging for decades and continue to release, polluting the atmosphere? A key question now is whether we can roll out an extensive programme of establishing and restoring native woodlands at a landscape scale rather than in small, isolated fragments. I wondered if this has ever been done before and, if so, how did it work out?

While previous centuries saw a relentless clearance of the native Irish forests, a relatively settled political period followed at the close of the seventeenth century with British dominance and the era of foreign landlords. The security offered to landed gentry encouraged them to plan for the long term and to invest in extensive tree planting. The Dublin Society, whose members were mostly large landowners, began to offer incentives for tree planting, insisting that new plantations should be fenced to exclude grazing animals or tree-cutting by the native Irish population. By 1744 the Society was offering grants for planting of oak, ash, elm, beech, walnut and chestnut but, as the century progressed, more exotic species crept into the picture, including firs, pines, larches, maples, sweet chestnut and many more experimental plantings. This was the age when European explorers and naturalists were scouring the known world for new species to bring back to their sponsors.

To see a collection of these species, I drove a short distance on back roads to the arboretum and National Botanic Gardens at Kilmacurragh which occupy a large estate near Wicklow town. The collection was started in 1722 and developed during the nineteenth century by Thomas Acton in conjunction with David Moore and his son Sir Frederick Moore, who were curators of the National Botanic Gardens at that time. Numerous plant species were collected from around the world being introduced to Ireland for the first time. The different soil and climatic conditions at Kilmacurragh resulted in many of these specimens succeeding here while struggling or failing at the National Botanic Gardens in Dublin City. Kilmacurragh is particularly famous for its conifers and rhododendron collections. Some of the trees here are centuries old. Native trees were not favoured but there is a yew tree here that was planted in the 1600s.

Although state planting in Ireland dates back to the start of the twentieth century, it might have begun two decades earlier when the British Prime Minister, William Gladstone, set up a commission to consider the possibilities of reafforestation in Ireland. By then the area under exotic American conifers had increased eightfold since the beginning of the nineteenth century.[122] In 1883, Daniel Howitz, a Danish forester, spent three months in Ireland. He had previously been a forest conservator in Australia and had advised the French government on afforestation in Algeria. After an extensive survey in Ireland, he came to the conclusion that five million acres (over 20,000 square kilometres), about a quarter of the land area in this country, was more suitable for forestry than any other land use. He proposed that 60 per cent of that should be on poor agricultural land along the western seaboard where he believed that forestry could provide work for the impoverished population, still suffering the after-effects of repeated famines. Of course, this took no account of the wishes of the people and the plan was never implemented. Interestingly, Howitz also proposed that a million acres (over 4,000 square kilometres) of forests could be planted in the main river basins to control soil erosion and runoff. Even two and a half centuries ago there was an understanding that extensive tree planting had significant benefits for water.

Political unrest in the early twentieth century meant that forestry as a business had essentially stalled. Due to the shortage of imported timber during the First World War there was an increase in felling and woodland acreage in Ireland was significantly reduced. However, by 1919 a new Forestry Act was passed in Ireland despite the ongoing War of Independence. Under the government of the new Irish Free State, forestry was assigned in 1922 to the Department of Lands and Agriculture. This gave a further boost to forestry with the intention of planting up to one or two million acres, thus creating a home-grown resource. In contrast to the previous rulers who saw forestry as a matter for private landowners, the new government proposed that most of the land would be state-owned and planted. At this time, land under forestry comprised less than 250,000 acres (about 1,000 square kilometres) with most of this in private hands. However, private landowners were generally unsympathetic to the proposals and refused to cooperate in the new enterprise preferring instead to neglect their woodlands thus depriving the country of these private forests and the knowledge and skills that had been accumulated in them over previous centuries.[123] The population of Ireland had been falling steadily since the Great Famine of the 1840s and the poverty that followed led to continuing emigration. There were many abandoned farms across the country but the land available for new forestry was mainly poor-quality wet soils, peatland or upland areas with the exception of some large lowland demesnes which had come into state hands.

After independence in the 1920s, there was continual debate about the merits of an ambitious reafforestation programme while experimentation with North American coniferous species was underway. However, it took until 1948 for the government to decide on a planting programme of 25,000 acres (about a hundred square kilometres) per year over forty years until the target of one million acres of new plantations had been established. At this stage over 14 per cent of the target had already been established in the new state and much of the land proposed for additional forestry was rough mountain grazing for sheep with generally poor peaty soils and high rainfall. In the years after 1950 large areas of land were acquired by the state for forestry planting and some of the earlier state plantations were reaching maturity. By 1959–60 the target rate of 25,000 acres (100 square kilometres) of planting per year was reached with the bulk of that in the poorest western counties. By 1960 almost 270,000 acres (1,100 square kilometres or about the size of County Longford) of new forests had been planted by the state, almost entirely composed of exotic conifers which were subsequently clear-felled.[124]

The amount of conifer forest planted by the state since 1922 showed that landscape-scale change was possible, although the targets of the post-war government were never achieved. However, by 1958 broadleaves comprised less than five per cent of state forests. The majority, Sitka spruce and lodgepole pine accounted for some three-quarters of the entire estate. The start of a movement to increase the cover of native broadleaved trees began in the late 1980s with the founding of the voluntary organisations Crann and the Tree Council of Ireland. At the same time, state forestry holdings were transferred to a new semi-state company, Coillte, which had commercial targets. Apart from the few fragments of semi-natural forest protected in national parks and nature reserves, the government's NPWS gave little attention to restoration of native woodland.

## People's Millennium Forests

A new drive to promote native woodland began in the late 1990s with the People's Millennium Forests Project. The target was to restore former native woodlands at a number of sites around the country and involve the Irish public directly in the project. This was to be achieved by protecting, enhancing and expanding native woodland through ongoing management. The sixteen sites were carefully selected – some were chosen because they were known to be relics of the native Irish forests of ancient times, while others were old woodland sites located in attractive amenity locations, with the potential to create valuable native woodlands.

Work on the selected woodlands commenced in 2000 and continues to the present day. The project is managed by Coillte, in partnership with Woodlands of Ireland, and was originally sponsored by AIB Bank, the National Millennium Committee and the Forest Service. Restoration of former native woodland cover in these areas has been achieved by removing non-native conifer trees that had been planted on some of the sites along with invasive shrubs such as rhododendron and cherry laurel. Over 1.3 million native trees and shrubs were planted and natural regeneration was encouraged where possible to restore some 500 hectares of woodland. The seeds used were collected from native woodlands in Ireland, and each sapling planted had been carefully nurtured at Coillte nurseries. Perimeter fencing was used to exclude grazing animals, particularly deer and livestock, an essential measure to protect the young planted trees.

Declan Little is the man who has guided and driven this project from the start as Project Manager for Woodlands of Ireland. Born and reared in Limerick, he trained in commercial horticulture and then became a soil scientist, a skill that he uses to this day to inform the planting of native woodland. Declan has been a key player in the movement to restore existing woodlands through better management. Along with colleagues, he has trained hundreds of foresters, ecologists and others in the best methods of woodland establishment and management. He travelled all over Ireland to advise landowners on the type of native woodland best suited to their property. Recently, he has moved to work as Lead Ecologist with Coillte Nature, currently part of the state-owned forestry company, bringing his extensive experience and network of contacts to a wider stage.

Coillte is also responsible for the day-to-day management of the People's Millennium Forests, where the young trees were each given a unique number. During the year 2000 every household in the country received a certificate outlining the registration number of their particular tree and where to go to locate it. The project team was asked to do this so that the people of Ireland would know that a tree was planted on behalf of each household in the restored woodlands. The message was simple – these native woodlands are for the people of Ireland. Every household in the country can identify with a particular native woodland in this project.

Now, some twenty years later, I am curious to see the place where our family's tree was planted and how this far-sighted initiative has progressed. So, I have made a visit to one of the Millennium forests at Ballygannon Wood near Rathdrum, County Wicklow. The Irish name of the wood, *Baile na gCanonach*, means 'the town or dwelling of the canons' as the church owned this land in the twelfth century. The wood later became part of the Watson-Wentworth estate. It had been managed under a coppice with standards system for 350 years. A large part of the woodland was cleared before 1750 and many more trees were cut down during the two world wars. Now the woods are mainly oak, holly, hazel and rowan, with bluebells and great woodrush growing on the sunlit forest floor. It is home to a typical selection of woodland birds with the interesting inclusion of the rare wood warbler. It also holds red squirrels, badgers, woodmice, shrews and foxes.

Today, Coillte is restoring Ballygannon as a working oakwood where conservation and timber production will eventually take place side by side. Over 40,000 oak trees, grown by Coillte from seeds collected in County Wicklow, have been planted here. Birch trees in the wood are being re-spaced also to allow the best-quality trees to grow bigger. Grazing animals like cattle, sheep, deer and rabbits will be kept out to conserve the trees and seedlings and allow them to spread. After two decades, the new trees are maturing fast and the canopy is merging with the older trees. It looks and feels like a natural woodland. The trees will grow and live for hundreds more years and bring pleasure to people now and long into the future.

However, the project is not without its challenges. According to Declan Little,

The results of long-term monitoring of vegetation (and beetles) at four of the People's Millennium Forests sites indicates that on all these sites, which

were cleared of conifers and where natural colonisation and succession is being observed, invasive
species and deer are having a negative impact. At
the species-poor site, in Cullentra, Co. Sligo, deer
numbers are high and woodland colonisation is
hampered severely by overgrazing. Rhododendron
is also a pernicious pest here and it is recommended that both these threats are managed
intensively.

These are problems faced by many woodlands
throughout the country and they need to be urgently
addressed on an ongoing basis.

### Farm woodlands

Agricultural land comprises almost two-thirds of the
Irish landscape with forests only about eleven per cent.
According to the Central Statistics Office, there are
137,500 farms in Ireland, the vast majority of which
are family-owned, with an average size of 32 hectares.
Many of these farms are small and fragmented units
that are struggling to provide a living for their owners
as agricultural economics favours large, industrial
farming. Hence, farmland in the poorer and wetter soils,

especially among the border counties and in the west
of Ireland, has become a target for forestry companies
wishing to invest in fast-growing trees. These areas also
offer the best prospect for native woodland restoration
as small-scale farming becomes increasingly non-viable.
Abandonment of farming in some areas for economic
reasons is also likely to lead to woodland development
by a process of natural succession, although this may
not be sustainable in the long term if pressure for food
production increases again.

I went to visit Ralph and Liz Sheppard's farm in east
Donegal which was originally a typical medium-sized
holding in this fertile corner of the county. The farm
was mainly grazed by cattle and sheep with some crops
but included a number of old trees in the hedgerows and
in an ancient wooded laneway that was once a bridle
path for people on horseback and those walking from
one settlement to another. At the bottom of the small
fields is the bank of the River Deele, overhung by large
alder and crack willow trees. In 1980, the owners fenced
off about half a hectare in a field corner and started
a mixed broadleaf plantation. The trees were mainly
oak, ash and birch with some alder, larch and Spanish
chestnut. The Sheppards were clear about their overall

objectives. They wanted to produce a commercial crop of timber as a future income. They also wanted to encourage nature by using native tree species to recreate a rich woodland ecosystem. And they wanted to enjoy it.

After ten years they had a healthy mixed plantation with some trees up to nine metres in height so they decided to plant another four hectares in a field left bare after harvesting a potato crop. Again, native species – oak, ash, cherry, alder and birch – dominated the planting with a few other broadleaves selected for their useful timber. As I walked through this woodland, now nearly thirty years old, I could see a delightful mix of different shapes and shades of trees with natural regeneration of typical woodland undergrowth. By the year 2000 the couple had selected another three-hectare field at the opposite end of the farm along the riverbank. This time they decided to use only native Irish trees – oak, ash, rowan, willow, alder, aspen, Scots pine, birch, hazel, cherry and crab apple. Now, almost twenty years later, the woodland is developing typical copses dominated by different heights of canopy with small clearings.

With three different ages of trees the Sheppards now have a native woodland maturing alongside their existing farm enterprise, enhancing the local landscape, providing them with a steady supply of fuel for heating their house and a surplus of timber for sale. As the trees mature, they use continuous cover methods to select and fell quality timber for high-value uses. They have gained much knowledge and skill in managing their woodlands and the innovative character of the project was recognised in 2005 with its selection by the Royal Dublin Society/Forest Service for a special Biodiverse Forest award. Ralph says, 'There are few things more positive than watching trees grow and managing them in a way that brings nature back to what had been fairly sterile farmland.' Here is an example of a careful conversion from farm to forest while providing income for the landowners.

Some landowners have a vision for their farms that is very different from the landscape that their prede-cessors managed. Christian Osthoff is the owner of a 50-hectare forest-farm in the rolling countryside of east Wicklow. Christian says:

> I was in the very fortunate position to have inherited the land from my mother, Elsa. She was the instigator of my passion for nature, its recording and conservation. She was also the

one who started the transition of the farm from predominantly grass-covered fields grazed by cattle and horses to a forest and wildlife haven.

When the initial moves were made in 1991 to plant 16 hectares, the forester suggested the whole lot should be Sitka spruce. For both Christian and his mother this was not how they wanted the farm to develop having seen quite enough of the Wicklow hills carpeted in this alien tree species over the years. Eventually, the plan changed and much of the farm was planted with mostly pedunculate oak and ash mixed with a wide variety of other species.

Since then, and at roughly five-year intervals, more blocks of trees have been added, to the point now where 38 hectares of the farm have been planted. Though still dominated by oak, the plantations now also include Spanish chestnut, beech, Norway spruce, Douglas fir, Scots pine, western red cedar, wild cherry and two species of larch, with an understorey of hazel, holly and other species. This succession of age classes fits in well with the 'close-to-nature' type of forestry management that is followed here. Clear-felling will never be the end goal.

I walked around the plantations with Mike Carswell, an experienced woodsman who has been managing the trees with Christian. Mike showed me the 28-year-old sweet chestnut that he has been thinning and the new deer fence that was constructed around it using poles made on site. The sun poured through the now open canopy and the ground was filled with bluebells. The original farm had many hedgerows with mature native trees and shrubs, including oak, beech, yew, spindle, Wych elm, guelder rose and an even rarer tree in Wicklow, the aspen. These have now been linked into the new maturing woodland. Mike has been coppicing some of the mature hazel plantations to return these to a seven-year rotation and in the process, produce a sustainable crop of hazel rods and pea sticks.

Christian is a keen wildlife observer and, over the years on his land, he has recorded twenty-one butterfly species, including silver-washed fritillary, wood white and even purple hairstreak, over 300 'macro' moth species, eighty-eight birds and twenty-one mammals, including five bats, red squirrel, otter, stoat and pine marten. Two large badger setts are well established in the woods. He received a grant from the Heritage Council to create two large ponds on some fallow ground he had reserved for this purpose by the river. He realised this was a habitat missing from the surrounding countryside, so he thought it would add greatly to the diversity of the farm. Within two years of their creation, Christian recorded twelve species of dragonflies and damselflies breeding on the ponds.

Five years ago, Christian built a timber-framed, energy-efficient, passive house on the farm. Much of the timber came from trees grown on the farm. Christian is also making a living providing fuelwood from his plantations, supplemented by his work as a cabinet-maker, for which he uses timber from his own woodlands. Recently he planted a fruit and berry orchard to feed himself and much wildlife besides. He has also established a large wildflower meadow to encourage pollinating insects. Here is a man who has a long-term vision to give something back to nature while managing his farm in the most environmentally sustainable way that he knows.

In 2016, the state agricultural research and advisory body, Teagasc, published a research paper on the potential availability of land for afforestation. To achieve a 'carbon neutral agriculture' by 2050, they concluded that planting would need to cover almost a fifth of the Republic. The current target set by the Irish government is to increase the forest cover to 18 per cent of the land area of the country by the year 2030. This will involve planting up large areas of existing or abandoned farmland but afforestation in recent years has fallen far short of the levels necessary to achieve this, despite the availability of substantial financial incentives. However, a recent study by Teagasc of farmer opinions found that the attitude of landowners to forestry was becoming more positive. The main reason for planting was the very favourable income from forestry premium payments on land that has limited other uses. Forestry was considered an alternative to agricultural enterprises on land that is marginal for farming or is situated some distance away from the main farmyard. The current challenge is to make long-term planting with native trees more attractive than the conventional short-rotation forestry.

In 2019, the Department of Agriculture launched three new measures to support biodiversity in Irish forests. One of the new schemes is to support continuous cover forestry, which allows for the production of commercial timber while retaining forest cover at all times. The other two measures were new deer tree shelter and deer and hare fencing schemes, which aim to prevent these browsing animals from damaging young plantations. These are encouraging moves for native woodland restoration but the central problem remains that broadleaf trees are seen as offering less commercial return than the annual supports for conventional agriculture.

## Reforesting the cutaway bogs

Since the midland bogs became mostly depleted of their peat supplies many of them have been allowed to revert to nature. The pumps that kept them dry are turned off, drains are allowed to become blocked and vegetation returns. At first, scrub develops – heather and gorse on the dryer areas, willows in the wet patches and reeds in the drains. Then the birch trees establish themselves and birchwoods grow across the landscape again. These are pioneer woodlands which will frequently be colonised by other more long-lived species such as oak, given time. Natural regeneration is the best way to restore the lost forests of Ireland as the species best suited to local conditions will find their own way back. This is rewilding in its purest form.

Long-established bog woodland is a rare and very distinctive habitat dominated by downy birch and

*Sphagnum* moss species. It can occur on active raised bogs, on cutaway bog and within sessile oak woodlands. In 2011 John Cross and Deirdre Lynn of the National Parks and Wildlife Service reported on the first year of monitoring at nine well-established bog woodlands of conservation value. All sites had good ecological structure and function but two sites were considered to have poor future prospects as one appeared to be drying out and the other was suffering from overgrazing preventing regeneration. Overall, the long-term future of old bog woodland sites is unclear as there is a possibility that these are naturally transient communities and may be simply a stage in succession to another habitat type such as raised bog or oak woodland.[125]

I have surveyed a number of these bog woodlands in County Cavan close to the border town of Belturbet. Most were in sites where the peat had been privately cut in the past but abandoned in the modern era leading to natural colonisation by birch woods. The damp atmosphere, sunlight shining through the small birch leaves and bark encrusted with lichens and mosses made it feel like some elves would soon appear from behind one of the trees. Bracken and birch normally spread in from the drier margins, eventually drying out the peat surface sufficiently to fill the wetter centre. Heather persists beneath the trees giving a strange mosaic of bog and woodland. Birch is a fast-growing species and it does best in wet acid soils. I imagine the turf cutters of old returning to find that the bog where they had worked as children was now covered with woodland.

In 2019, Bord na Móna and Coillte announced a joint initiative which will see approximately 600,000 native trees being established over three years across 1,500 hectares of cutaway bog that is no longer used for peat production. The focus is on accelerating native woodland cover, where appropriate, on the drier bog areas above the high flood/waterline. A mix of native Irish trees, mainly pioneer woodland species such as downy birch, alder, willow, rowan and Scots pine, will be planted with smaller amounts of shrubs such as hazel, holly and spindle. Bord na Móna lands identified for the project are in counties Offaly, Laois, Westmeath and Tipperary. Teams from Coillte Nature and Bord na Móna will work together to provide the management, forestry, nursery and technical expertise to establish and maintain the woodlands. This native woodland project is to be integrated with Bord na Móna's extensive peatland rehabilitation and bog restoration programme that will see a total of 35,000 hectares of peatland rehabilitated by 2025 contributing significantly to the capture of carbon from the atmosphere.

### Ireland's role in the global effort

The climate crisis is overwhelmingly the most important reason for expanding the area under forest. Swiss university researchers estimate that a worldwide planting programme could remove two-thirds of all the greenhouse gases that have been released to the atmosphere since the Industrial Revolution. A team, led by Jean-François Bastin at ETH Zurich, mapped the global potential tree coverage to show that 4.4 billion hectares of canopy cover could potentially exist under the current climate. Excluding existing trees and agricultural and urban areas, they found that there is room for almost an extra billion hectares of canopy cover, which could store 205 gigatonnes of carbon in areas that would naturally support woodlands and forests. However, things are not static and current trends in climate change will alter this potential tree coverage. As most of the short-term changes are already inevitable, the global potential canopy cover may shrink by about 223 million hectares by 2050, with the vast majority of losses occurring in the tropics. These results highlight the opportunity provided by climate change to restore large areas of natural vegetation to the globe.[126]

This debate has only just begun with an immediate response by Robin Chazdon of the USA and Pedro Brancalion of Brazil. They point out that using only the biophysical capacity for restoring global tree cover is insufficient for evaluating where forests can be feasibly increased. The kinds of trees, as well as how and where they are grown, determine how and which people benefit and these factors also need to be taken into account. They warn that increasing tree cover can elevate fire risk, decrease water supplies and cause crop damage by wildlife. Reforestation programs often favour single-species tree plantations over restoring native forest ecosystems. This approach can generate negative consequences for biodiversity and carbon storage, threaten food and land security, and exacerbate social inequities.[127]

Ireland covers a tiny part of the globe but, if this country is really serious about responding to the climate and biodiversity crisis, we will need to turn large areas over to forests in future. The political moves to bring this about have already begun but they are far from adequate. A fundamental shift in forestry policy was proposed in 2019 by the Green Party, moving away from heavy reliance on conifers towards a focus on native woodlands. The party called for the government to push for a more diverse continuous cover forestry model, supporting a wider range of forest types including semi-wild areas and forestry on farms. The current clear-fell plantation model is dominated by conifer production. If adopted as government policy, the Green Party's proposals would have far-reaching consequences for the state-owned companies Coillte and Bord na Móna, which between them own the largest land block in the country. A rebalancing of forest premiums and payments to support this strategic shift would be necessary. The Green Party wants to allow for restoration of large areas of permanent natural woodlands – including new grants so every farmer could grow a special hectare of native woodlands over the next five years. The government recently outlined a new planting target of 22 million trees every year for the next 20 years with short-rotation conifer plantations accounting for 70 per cent of new afforestation, with the remaining 30 per cent being broadleaf trees. Clearly, this will help in the response to climate change but it will not do enough to reverse the centuries of loss in woodland biodiversity.

### Community woodlands

There is no reason why all of the reforestation effort in Ireland should be solely the responsibility of the government. The introduction of grants is primarily targeted at private landowners, farmers and others to plant trees on their own land. But there is another way that deserves discussion. Woodlands planned and/or managed in co-operation with local communities can engender a caring culture locally towards woodlands and the environment generally.

Community forestry has been practised for many years in the developing world and some western European countries. This allows a more localised, decentralized approach to landscape and forest restoration and care which has also been adopted more recently in North America. It involves managing the forests with the primary objective of benefiting neighbouring communities. Three main attributes characterise most community forest projects. Local residents start by protecting and restoring the forest. They have access to the land for a variety of purposes and they participate in decisions concerning the management of the forest for their own long-term benefit.[128]

In British Columbia the concept of community forestry is well established and widely accepted by the population as a whole. The Community Forest Agreement Program was initiated there in 1998. Under this scheme, a wide range of organisations have been recognised as 'communities': First Nations, municipal governments, environmental non-profits, local societies and cooperatives, and partnerships between various combinations of these groups have all been granted tenures under the program. In stark comparison with Canada, proposals for community forestry on federal lands in the USA have been met with strong opposition from major environmental organisations. There has been much heated argument in Congress, the media and academic journals about the acceptability of this approach and the views of Native Americans and labour representatives have been largely absent from these discussions.[129]

In Germany, community forestry was first introduced during the eighteenth century when village cooperatives shared common property including forests. Although they are now also owned by cities or rural communes, every person in the community is formally an owner of the forest, without there being a specific area assigned to each. All members have access to the forest and its products and may partake in decision-making regarding management. A recent study has shown that these community forests are sustainably managed and generally beneficial to nature. While their very longevity is some measure of success it seems that powerful actors usually control their management. The direct forest user is little involved and benefits only slightly.[130]

In England, the idea of community forests grew out of a focus on urban forestry in the 1980s. These woodlands were often established by local authorities, with support from the Forestry Commission, to rehabilitate former industrial or mining lands and provide improved recreational opportunities for deprived communities. By contrast, in Scotland community forestry is defined by community ownership of woodlands, or community control over woodland decision-making. Many of these communities want local assets to generate local benefits, especially employment. There is a risk that the state can crowd out existing community engagement, and there is a need to facilitate community empowerment without official agencies working 'on their behalf'.[131]

In Ireland, there is already a grant scheme called NeighbourWood which supports community groups in partnership with local authorities, Coillte or the NPWS. This is used to fund the management of woods that can be used by local people, often daily, for a host of outdoor recreational activities. Local schools often use them as an 'outdoor classroom' where young people can learn about nature and the environment. An example is FitzSimon's Wood in Sandyford, Dublin where representatives of the neighbouring housing estate became involved in a Friends of the Wood group. Owned by Dún Laoghaire Rathdown County Council, improvements to this native woodland were carried out in 2008 assisted by the NeighbourWood grant scheme. There were surveys of the habitats and mammals in the wood. Native trees were planted although some of these were lost due to deer grazing. A nature trail was planned here so I went for a walk around it to see some of the local wildlife.

Some sections of the wood have old trees that probably date from at least the 1830s but most of the trees are much younger because the woodland was repeatedly exploited for its timber. Birch is the commonest tree in the woodland and there are small areas of other habitats such as meadows, heathland and a stream. The wood has a surprisingly wild atmosphere despite its proximity to the built-up areas of the capital city and there was plenty of evidence that local children were using it as a playground.

However, with a NeighbourWood scheme there are no commercial or employment benefits and the members of the community group have no financial stake in the development of the wood which might ensure its long-term protection. Even so, an outdoor amenity such as this brings many other less tangible benefits to local communities and helps to nurture their interest in woodland restoration.

In a recent development, Coillte Nature has announced that it will gradually convert a total of nine commercial forests in the Dublin Mountains to native and mixed woodlands. This will involve a mixture of conventional tree-felling and replanting with native tree species, continuous cover forestry and long-term retention of other tree species. It will be done over the next thirty to forty years providing greater habitat variety for native wildlife and enhanced opportunities for outdoor recreation such as hill-walking, mountain biking and orienteering.

## Past and future

At the start of the nineteenth century, Ned's grand-father settled down to run the farm that includes our woodland. By the 1920s when the farm was finally sold, his family had occupied this place for four generations. During all that time, the oak trees along the road grew steadily and were only reaching maturity a century later when my own family took over stewardship of the land. Hopefully, the trees will live on here for several hundred more years as the world around them changes beyond recognition.

We intend to do our bit on the small piece of land that Ned once owned. We are managing the existing mature woodland here to maximise its biodiversity, providing a refuge for some sensitive woodland species that will ultimately recolonise surrounding areas of countryside as the forest habitat expands. Some of the fields, where Ned grew oats and potatoes, have been returned to management as species-rich meadows. On the rest of the land we have already planted a signif-icant proportion with native trees, protecting these from grazing animals while they are vulnerable. This plantation links with the old woodland, creating a corridor through which wildlife can move to other fragments of tree cover in the area. To support new woodland planting schemes elsewhere we have also established a native tree nursery using tree seed such as acorns and hazelnuts collected from local wild sources and grown to healthy young saplings.

This work is practical and satisfying. I will see some progress in my lifetime and my children and grand-children will benefit from the growing resource, from living and working in more natural surroundings and by knowing that they are making a real contribution to reversing the climate and biodiversity crisis that we have all created. Apart from the purely utilitarian benefits, I enjoy working outdoors in nature and take inspiration from the trees and the wildlife that they support. I will use this project to educate and influence people, to regard native woodland as one of the best ways to restore our green and pleasant land. If I believed in rebirth, I would love to return in another century to see if the trees that we planted now form a fine oakwood in its prime.

I sit alone by the fire in the wood listening to the bubbling sounds of the river beside me. I usually celebrate the winter solstice with a breakfast cooked over the glowing embers. I think about all that had happened since the last year's turning. From the first leaf burst to the final fall of foliage, all the trees have grown another two rings in their wood. Some old trees did not make it through the year, but even as they decay on the woodland floor, they continue to support a diverse community of small creatures. The breeding woodpeckers have gone for the winter, but their choice of this wood for their home shows me that nature can find a way back. Our own work in the wood is starting to show results. There are sunlit clearings with bright woodland flowers in spring and regenerating oaks and hazels. We have a large supply of hazelnuts and a woodstore stacked high with seasoned firewood that will keep the house warm through the winter.

The pioneering American naturalist John Muir wrote, 'The clearest way into the universe is through a forest wilderness.' I realise that our woodland has helped me to value the important things – family, environment and contentment with life.

# References

**INTRODUCTION**

1     Connolly, M. (2017). *Aghoule – Where the Divil ate the Tinker: The history of a Wicklow townland and its farming community.* Dublin: Applefield Publishing.

2     Connolly, M. (2017). *ibid.*

3     Perrin, P., James Martin, J., Barron, S., O'Neill, F., McNutt, K. and Delaney, A. (2008) *National Survey of Native Woodlands 2003–2008.* Dublin: National Parks and Wildlife Service.

**WINTER – SLEEPING TREES**

4     Wyse Jackson, P. (2014). *Ireland's Generous Nature: The past and present uses of wild plants in Ireland.* St Louis: Missouri Botanical Garden.

5     Niemann, D. (2016). *A Tale of Trees: The battle to save Britain's Ancient Woodland.* London: Short Books.

6     Rackham, O. (1995). 'Looking for ancient woodland in Ireland'. In: Pilcher, J.R. and Mac an tSaoir, S.S. (eds) *Wood, trees and forests in Ireland.* Dublin: Royal Irish Academy, pp. 1–12.

7     Weld, I. (1807). *Illustrations of the scenery of Killarney and surrounding country.*

8    Mitchell, F.J.G. (1990). 'The history and vegetation dynamics of
     a yew wood (*Taxus baccata* L.) in S.W. Ireland'. *New Phytologist*
     115, pp. 573–577.

9    Mitchell, F.J.G. (1995). 'The dynamics of Irish post-glacial forests'.
     In: Pilcher, J.R. and Mac an tSaoir, S.S. (eds) *Woods, trees and
     forests in Ireland*. Dublin. Royal Irish Academy.

10   Nairn, R., Jeffrey, D. and Goodbody, R. (2017). *Dublin Bay:
     nature and history*. Cork: Collins Press.

11   Cooney, G. (2000). *Landscapes of Neolithic Ireland*. London:
     Routledge

12   Everett, N. (2014). *The woods of Ireland: a history, 700–1800*.
     Dublin: Four Courts Press.

13   Hayes, S. (1974). *Treatise on planting and the management of
     woods and coppices*. Facsimile edition, published 2003 by Dublin:
     New Island Press, Dublin.

14   Carey, M. (2009). *If trees could talk – Wicklow's trees and
     woodlands over four centuries*. Dublin: Coford.

15   Alexander, K.N.A. (2011). 'An invertebrate survey of Coill Eoin,
     St John's Wood, Co Roscommon'. *Irish Wildlife Manuals No. 57*.
     Dublin: National Parks and Wildlife Service.

16   Corcoran, A. (2007). *Relationships between coppice management
     and biological diversity in an Irish ancient semi-natural
     woodland*. MSc Thesis. University College Dublin.

17   Clarke, M. (1988). *Badgers*. London: Whittet Books.

18   Smal, C.M. (1995). *The badger and habitat survey of Ireland*.
     Dublin: The Stationery Office.

19   Reid, N., Etherington, T.R., Wilson, G., McDonald, R.A.
     and Montgomery, W.I. 2008. *Badger survey of Northern
     Ireland 2007/08*. Report prepared by Quercus and Central
     Science Laboratory for the Department of Agriculture & Rural
     Development (DARD), Northern Ireland, UK.

20   Ham, C., Donnelly, C.A., Astley, K.L., Jackson, S.Y.B. and
     Woodroffe, R. (2019). 'Effect of culling on individual badger
     *Meles meles* behaviour: potential implications for bovine
     tuberculosis transmission'. *Journal of Applied Ecology* 00,
     pp. 1–10.

21   Hayden, T. and Harrington, R. (2000). *Exploring Irish mammals.* Dublin: Town House and Country House.

22   Joyce, P.W. (1968). *Irish Local Names Explained.* Dublin: Fred Hanna Ltd.

23   Perrin *et al.* (2008). *op.cit.*

24   Higgins, G.T. (2008). '*Rhododendron ponticum*: a guide to management on nature conservation sites'. *Irish Wildlife Manuals*, No. 33. Dublin: National Parks and Wildlife Service, Department of the Environment, Heritage and Local Government.

25   Fogarty, P. (2017). *Whittled Away: Ireland's vanishing nature.* Cork: The Collins Press.

26   HSE (2018). 'Seasonal Affective Disorder'. Available at: https://www2.hse.ie/conditions/mental-health/seasonal-affective-disorder/seasonal-affective-disorder-sad-symptoms.html

27   Marshall, R. (2003). *Celebrating Irish festivals.* Stroud, Gloucester: Hawthorn Press.

28   Makins, F.K. (1946). *British trees in winter.* London: Dent and Sons.

29   Gooley, T. (2012). *The Natural Navigator: the rediscovered art of letting nature be your guide.* New York. Barnes and Noble.

30   Stobart, A. (2020). *The medicinal forest garden handbook.* East Meon, Hampshire: Permanent Publications.

31   Speight, M.C.D. (1985). 'The extinction of indigenous *Pinus sylvestris* in Ireland: relevant faunal data'. *Irish Naturalists' Journal* 21, pp. 449–53.

32   Roche, J.R., Mitchell, F.J.G., Waldren, S. and Bjørndalen, J.E. (2015). 'Are Ireland's reintroduced *Pinus sylvestris* forests floristically analogous to their native counterparts in oceanic north-west Europe?' *Biology and Environment: Proceedings of the Royal Irish Academy* 115, pp. 1–18.

33   Roche J.R. (2010). *The vegetation ecology and native status of Scots pine (*Pinus sylvestris L.*) in Ireland.* Ph.D. Thesis, Trinity College Dublin.

34   Little, D. and Cross, J. (2005) *Realising quality qood from Ireland's native woodlands.* Dublin: Woodlands of Ireland.

35    Pukkala, T. and von Gadow, K. (eds) (2012) *Managing Forest
      Ecosystems, Vol. 23: Continuous Cover Forestry*. Dordrecht
      Heidelberg London New York: Springer.

36    Farjon, A. and Hill, L. (2019). Natural woodland generation as an
      alternative to tree-planting. *British Wildlife* 30, pp. 177–85.

37    Löf, M., Castro, J., Engman, M., Leverkus, A.B., Madsen, P.,
      Reque, J.A., Villalobos, A. and Gardiner, E.S. (2019). Tamm
      Review: direct seeding to restore oak *(Quercus* spp.) forests and
      woodlands. *Forest Ecology and Management* 448, pp. 474–89.

38    Watson, H.C. (1847–1859). *Cybele Britannica*. London: Longman
      & Co.

39    Webb, D.A. (1885). What are the criteria for presuming native
      species? *Watsonia* 15, pp. 231–6.

40    Cross, J. (2012). *Ireland's woodland heritage*. Dublin: Department
      of Arts, Heritage and the Gaeltacht.

41    Kelly, F. (1999). Trees in early Ireland. *Irish Forestry*

42     Potzelsberger, E. (no date). *Should we be afraid of non-native
      trees in our forests?* Vienna: University of Natural Resources and
      Life Sciences.

**SPRING — RISING SAP**

43    Donkersley, P. (2019). 'Trees for bees'. *Agriculture, Ecosystems
      and Environment* 270–271, pp. 79–83.

44    All-Ireland Pollinator Plan. Available at: https://pollinators.ie/

45    Mulcahy, R. (1996). *For love of trees: trees, hedgerows, ivy and
      the environment*. Dublin: Environmental Publications.

46    Rackham, O. (1976). *Trees and woodland in the British
      landscape*. London: J.M. Dent.

47    Collis, J.S. (1973). *The worm forgives the plough*. London.
      Jonathan Cape.

48    Mapes, L.V. (2019). *Witness tree: seasons of change with a
      century-old oak*. Seattle: University of Washington Press.

49    Sparks, T., Whittle, L. and Garforth, J. (2020). 'A comparison
      of Nature's Calendar with Gilbert White's phenology'. *British
      Wildlife* 31, pp. 271–275.

50    Viney, M. (1996). 'Watching for bud burst'. *Irish Times*. 16 March 1996.

51    Leech, D.I and Crick, H.Q.P. (2007). 'Influence of climate change on the abundance, distribution and phenology of woodland bird species in temperate regions'. *Ibis* 149 (Suppl. 2), pp. 128–45.

52    Mitchell, F. (1976). *The Irish landscape*. London: Collins.

53    Mitchell, F.J.G. (2008). 'Tree migration into Ireland'. In: Davenport, J.L., Sleeman, D.L. and Woodman, P.C. (eds). *Mind the gap: Post-glacial colonization of Ireland*. Special supplement to the *Irish Naturalists' Journal*, pp. 73–5.

54    Rackham, O. (2006). *Woodlands: new naturalist*. London: Harper Collins.

55    Tansley, A.G. (1939). *The British Islands and their vegetation*. Cambridge: Cambridge University Press.

56    Vera, F. (2000). *Grazing ecology and forest history*. Wallingford: CABI.

57    Sielmann, H. (1959). *My year with the woodpeckers*. London: Barrie and Rockliff.

58    Scharff, R.F., Ussher, R.J., Cole, G.A.J., Newton, E.T., Dixon, A.F and Westropp, T.J. (1906). 'The exploration of the caves of County Clare'. *Transactions of the Royal Irish Academy* 33B: 1–76.

59    Kelly Quinn, M. (1994). 'The evolution of forestry in County Wicklow from prehistory to the present'. In: Ken Hannigan & William Nolan (eds), *Wicklow History & Society*. Dublin: Geography Publications.

60    Coombes, R.H. and Wilson, F.R. (2015). 'Colonisation and breeding status of the Great Spotted Woodpecker *Dendrocopus major* in the Republic of Ireland'. *Irish Birds* 10, pp. 183–96.

61    Nairn, R. and Farrelly, P. (1991). 'Breeding bird communities of broadleaved woodland in the Glen of the Downs, Co. Wicklow'. *Irish Birds* 4, pp. 377–92.

62    Yapp. W.B. (1962). *Birds and woods*. London: Oxford University Press.

63    Sweeney, O., Kelly, T.C., Irwin, S., Wilson, M. and O'Halloran, J. (2012). Woodlands, Forest and Scrub. In: Richard Nairn and John O'Halloran (eds), *Bird Habitats in Ireland*. Cork: Collins Press.

64    Colm (2013). *Sacred trees in early Ireland*. IrishArchaeology.ie

65    Wolfe, L.M. (1979). *John of the mountains*. Madison: University of Wisconsin Press.

SUMMER — FOREST FLOWERING

66    Lysaght, L. and Marnell, F. (2016). *The atlas of mammals in Ireland 2010–2015*. Waterford: National Biodiversity Centre.

67    Purser, P., Wilson, F. and Carden, R. (2009). *Deer and forestry in Ireland: a review of current status and management requirements*. Report to Woodlands of Ireland.

68    Höna, S., Nugent, C., Burkitt, T. and Little. D. (2018). The management of deer in native woodlands. *Woodlands of Ireland, Native Woodland Information Note No. 7*, pp. 1–35.

69    O'Connell, M. (1994). *Connemara: Vegetation and land use since the last Ice Age*. Dublin: Office of Public Works.

70    Cooney, G. (2000). *op. cit.*

71    Cooney, G. (2000). *ibid.*

72    Aalen, F.H.A., Whelan, K. and Stout, M. (eds.) (1997). *Atlas of the Irish rural landscape*. Cork: Cork University Press.

73    Cooney, G. (2000). *op. cit.*

74    O'Meara J.J. (1982). *Giraldus Cambrensis: The history and topography of Ireland translated from the Latin*. Portlaoise: The Dolmen Press.

75    Osbourne, L.L. and Kovacic, D.A. (1993). 'Riparian vegetated buffer strips in water-quality restoration and stream management'. *Freshwater Biology* 29, pp. 243–58.

76    Weigelhofer, G., Fuchsberger, J., Teufl, B., Welti, N. and Hein, T. (2012). 'Effects of riparian forest buffers on in-stream nutrient retention in agricultural catchments'. *Journal of Environmental Quality* 41, pp. 373–9.

77    Vera (2000). *op. cit.*

78   O'Mahony, D.T., Powell, C., Power, J., Hannify, R., Turner, P. and O' Reilly, C. (2017). 'National pine marten population assessment 2016'. *Irish Wildlife Manuals*, No. 97. Dublin: National Parks and Wildlife Service, Department of the Arts, Heritage, Regional, Rural and Gaeltacht Affairs.

79   Rackham, O. (2014). *The ash tree*. Dorset: Little Toller Books.

80   McCoitir, N. (2003). *Irish trees: myths, legends and folklore*. Cork: The Collins Press.

81   Mitchell, R.J. *et al.* (2017). 'Challenges in assessing the ecological impacts of tree diseases and mitigation measures: the case of *Hymenoscyphus fraxinus* and *Fraxinus excelsior*'. *Baltic Forestry* 23, pp. 116–40.

82   Qing L. (2018). *Shinrin-Yoku: The Art and Science of Forest Bathing*. London: Penguin Life.

83   Ambrose-Oji, B. (2013). *Mindfulness practice in woods and forests: an evidence review*. Research Report for The Mersey Forest, Forest Research. Alice Holt Lodge Farnham, Surrey.

84   Wyse Jackson, P. (2014). *op.cit.*

85   Rutty, J. (1772). *An essay towards a natural history of the County of Dublin*. Volume 1. Dublin: Sleater.

86   Wyse Jackson, P. (2014). *op.cit.*

## AUTUMN – FRUITS OF THE FOREST

87   Dowding, P. and Smith, L. (2011) *Forest Fungi in Ireland*. Dublin: Coford.

88   Mabey, R. (1972). *Food for Free*. London: Collins.

89   Woodman, P.C. (2014). Ireland's native mammals: a survey of the archaeological record. In: D.P. Sleeman, J. Carlsson and J.E.L. Carlsson (eds), *Mind the gap II: New insights into the Irish postglacial*. Belfast: Irish Naturalists' Journal.

90   Lewis-Stemple, J. (2009). *The wild life: A year of living on wild food*. London: Doubleday.

91   Wyse Jackson, P. (2014). *op.cit.*

92   Curtis, T. and Whelan, P. (2019). *The wild food plants of Ireland*. Cork: Orla Kelly Publishing.

93    Ó Cléirín, C. and Ó Cléirín, K. (1978). *Wild and free: cooking from nature*. Dublin: O'Brien Press.

94    Wyse Jackson, P. (2014). *op.cit.*

95    Wyse Jackson, P. (2014). *op.cit.*

96    McCracken, E. (1971). *The Irish woods since Tudor times*. Newton Abbott: David and Charles.

97    Rackham, O. (1995). *op.cit.*

98    Hall, V.A. (1995). Woodland depletion in Ireland over the last millennium. In: Pilcher, J.R. and Mac an tSaoir, S.S. (eds), *Woods, trees and forests in Ireland*. Dublin: Royal Irish Academy.

99    Kelly, D.L. and Fuller, S. (1988). Ancient woodland in central Ireland: does it exist? In: F. Salbitano (ed.) *Human influence on forest ecosystems development in Europe*, pp. 363–369.

100   Peterken, G.F. and Mountford, E.P. (2005). 'Natural woodland reserves: 60 years of trying at Lady Park Wood'. *British Wildlife* 17, pp. 7–16.

101   Little, D. (2019). 'The wilderness concept: Ireland, native woodlands and woodlands of Ireland'. Unpublished discussion paper. Woodlands of Ireland.

102   Sharkey, N., Jones, M. and Bourke, D. (2013). 'Climate change impacts on woodland species: implications for the conservation of woodland habitats in Ireland'. *Biology and Environment: Proceedings of the Royal Irish Academy* 113B, pp. 227–257.

103   Monbiot, G. (2013). *Feral: rewilding the land, sea and human life*. London: Penguin.

104   Hickey, K. (2011). *Wolves in Ireland: a natural and cultural history*. Dublin: Four Courts Press.

105   Hickey (2011). *ibid.*

106   Perrin et al. (2008). *op. cit.*

107   Wohlleben, P. (2016). *The Hidden Life of Trees*. Vancouver/Berkeley: Greystone Books.

108   Wyse Jackson, P. (2014). *op.cit.*

109   Dowding, P. and Smith, L. (2011). *op.cit.*

110   Keator, G. and Bazell, S. (1998). *The life of an oak: an intimate portrait*. Berkeley: Heyday Books and the California Oak Foundation.

111 Logan, W.B. (2005). *Oak: the frame of civilization*. New York: Norton & Company.

112 Mapes, L.V. (2019). *op.cit.*

113 Mitchell, R.J., Bellamy, P.E., Ellis, C.J., Hewison, R.L., Hodgetts, N.G., Iason, G.R., Littlewood, N.A., Newey, S., Stockan, J.A., Taylor, A.F.S. (2019). 'Oak-associated biodiversity in the UK (OakEcol)'. *NERC Environmental Information Data Centre*. https://www.hutton.ac.uk/oak-decline.

114 Fennessy, J. (2002). 'The collection, storage, treatment and handling of broadleaved tree seed'. *Coford Connects. Reproductive Material* No. 4, pp. 1–6.

115 Wyse Jackson, P. (2014). *op.cit.*

116 Louv, R. (2009). *Last child in the woods: saving our children from nature-deficit disorder*. London: Atlantic Books.

117 Langston, N. (1995). *Forest Dreams, Forest Nightmares: the paradox of old growth in the inland west*. Seattle: University of Washington Press.

**FUTURE FORESTS – LONG LIFE**

118 Barrow, E. (2019). *Our future in nature: trees, spirituality and ecology*. Bloomington: Balboa Press.

119 Aalen, F.H.A., Whelan, K. and Stout, M. (eds) (1997). *Atlas of the Irish rural landscape*. Cork: Cork University Press.

120 Keith, H., Mackey, B.G. and Lindenmayer, D.B. (2009). Re-evaluation of forest biomass carbon stocks and lessons from the world's most carbon-dense forests. *Proceedings of the National Academy of Sciences* 106, pp. 11635–40.

121 Leuzinger, S., Zotz, G., Asshoff, R. and Korner, C. (2005). Responses of deciduous forest trees to severe drought in Central Europe. *Tree Physiology* 25, pp. 641–50.

122 McCracken, E. (1971). *op.cit.*

123 Neeson, E. (1991). *A history of Irish forestry*. Dublin: Lilliput Press.

124 Neeson, E. *ibid.*

125    Cross, J. and Lynn, D. (2013). 'Results of a monitoring survey of
       bog woodland'. *Irish Wildlife Manuals, No. 69*. Dublin: National
       Parks and Wildlife Service, Department of Arts, Heritage and the
       Gaeltacht.

126    Bastin, J-F., Finegold, Y., Garcia C., Mollicone, D., Rezende, M.,
       Routh, D., Zohner, C.M. and Crowther, T. (2019). 'The global
       tree restoration potential'. *Science* 365, pp. 76–9.

127    Chazdon, R. and Brancalion, P. (2019). 'Restoring forests as a
       means to many ends'. *Science* 365 (6448), pp. 24–25.

128    Brendler, T. and Carey, H. (1998). 'Community forestry, defined'.
       *Journal of Forestry*, 96(3), pp. 21–3.

129    McCarthy, J. (2006). 'Neoliberalism and the politics of
       alternatives: community forestry in British Columbia and
       the United States'. *Annals of the Association of American
       Geographers*, 96(1), pp. 84–104.

130    Schusser, C., Krott, M., Logmani, J., Sadath, N., Movuh, M. C.
       Y. and Salla, M. (2013). 'Community Forestry in Germany, a case
       study seen through the lens of the international model'. *Journal of
       Sustainable Development*, 6(9), pp. 88–100.

131    Lawrence, A., Anglezarke, B., Frost, B., Nolan, P. and Owen, R.
       (2009). 'What does community forestry mean in a devolved Great
       Britain?' International Forestry Review 11(2), pp. 281–97.